Gardens
of British Columbia

Gardens
of British Columbia

An Altitude SuperGuide by Pat Kramer

Publication Information

Altitude Publishing Canada Ltd.
The Canadian Rockies
1500 Railway Avenue
Canmore, Alberta T1W 1P6

Copyright 1998 © Pat Kramer

Extreme care has been taken to ensure that all information presented in this book is accurate and up-to-date, and neither the author nor the publisher can be held responsible for any errors.

Canadian Cataloguing in Publication Data
Kramer, Pat
Gardens of British Columbia
Includes bibliographical references
ISBN 1-55153-620-X
1. Gardens —British Columbia. I. Title.
SB466.C32B7 1998   635'.09711   C98-910448-6

Made in Western Canada
Printed and bound in Western Canada by Friesen Printers, Altona, Manitoba.

Altitude GreenTree Program
Altitude Publishing will plant in Western Canada twice as many trees as were used in the manufacturing of this product.

Photographs
Front cover: The Butchart Gardens
Inset: Butterfly
Inset: Tea cup
Frontispieces: Park and Tilford Garden, North Vancouver; Pink tulip
Back cover: VanDusen Botanical Garden

Project Development
Concept/art direction	Stephen Hutchings
Design/layout	Kelly Stauffer
Editor	Sabrina Grobler
Index	Noeline Bridge
Financial management	Laurie Smith
Sales management	Scott Davidson

A Note from the Publisher
The world described in *Altitude SuperGuides* is a unique and fascinating place. It is a world filled with surprise and discovery, beauty and enjoyment, questions and answers. It is a world of people, cities, landscape, animals and wilderness as seen through the eyes of those who live in, work with, and care for this world. The process of describing this world is also a means of defining ourselves.

It is also a world of relationship, where people derive their meaning from a deep and abiding contact with the land—as well as from each other. And it is this sense of relationship that guides all of us at Altitude to ensure that these places continue to survive and evolve in the decades ahead.

Altitude SuperGuides are books intended to be used, as much as read. Like the world they describe, *Altitude SuperGuides* are evolving, adapting and growing. Please write to us with your comments and observations, and we will do our best to incorporate your ideas into future editions of these books.

Stephen Hutchings
Publisher

Contents

The Gardens of British Columbia are organized according to this colour scheme:

Introduction

Greater Victoria

Vancouver Island

Greater Vancouver

Fraser Valley

B.C. Interior

Reference and Index

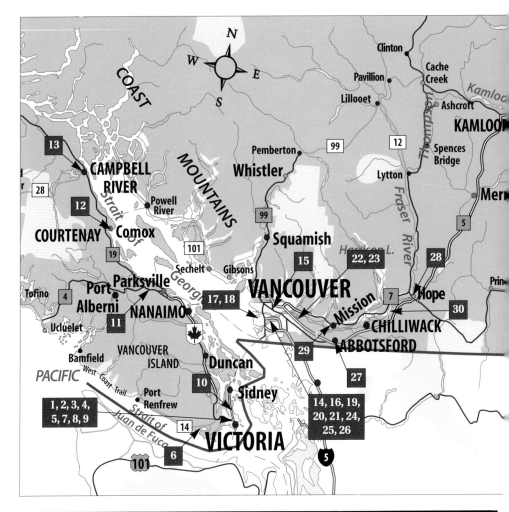

The gardens that appear on this map are located according to the number that preceeds them in the list below. For further information, please refer to the page numbers that follow each garden, also listed.

Greater Victoria
1. Ann Hathaway's Cottage Garden, p. 15
2. The Butchart Gardens, p. 21
3. Craigflower House Heritage Gardens, p. 28
4. Crystal Garden, p. 31
5. Government House Gardens, p. 33
6. Hatley Castle Park Gardens (Sooke), p. 35
7. Knot Garden, p. 41
8. Point Ellice House Heirloom Gardens, p. 47
9. Undersea Gardens, p. 57
10. Butterfly Gardens, p. 58

Vancouver Island
11. Butterfly World (Coombs), p. 64
12. Filburg Lodge and Gardens (Comox), p. 66
13. Haig-Brown House and Gardens
    (Cambell River), p. 67

Greater Vancouver
14. Arthur Erickson's Garden, p. 70
15. Century Gardens (Burnaby), p. 73
16. Dr. Sun-Yat-Sen Classical Chinese Garden, p. 76
17. Fantasy Garden World (Richmond), p. 80

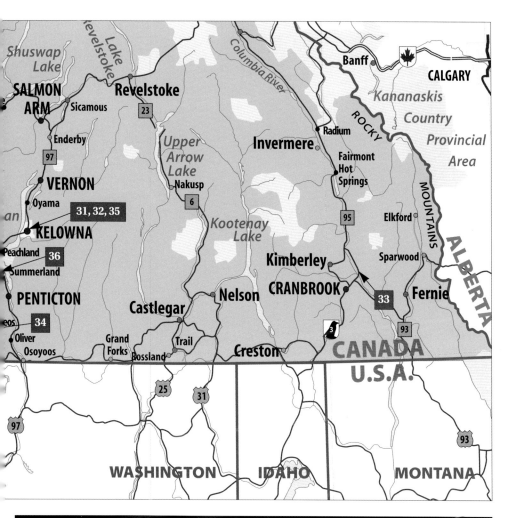

Gardens in B.C

About This Book

Garden lovers are down-to-earth people. It goes with the territory. It is only natural then, to enjoy British Columbia's show gardens in the presence of its many aficionados. A quick glance at the Special Features, reveals myriads of B.C. garden discoveries just steps away. Forget about seed catalogues and fertilizer problems for a while, and enjoy the tales that describe this western province's garden heritage. This book is about garden festivals, garden lore, garden history, garden visits and the reason British Columbia is renowned for its gardens. It is about appreciating garden style and getting to know the dynamic people who, for the last 150 years, have quietly created wondrous places in the midst of spectacular mountain and ocean settings. Each garden has its own magic and its own story to tell. Not only will these chapters open your eyes to the splendours of Western Canadian floral beauty, they explore British Columbia's role in the evolution of one of humankind's oldest ventures. For what is a garden without its roots?

This book can be read on many levels. Dip into it anywhere you like. You can revel in the horticultural heritage of B.C.'s many immigrants, or you can plan a garden-touring adventure among showy displays of spring and summer flowers. If you want to know more about established garden traditions, quick background research is available here. From traditional old Victorian rose gardens to to-

Butterflies add to the entertainment of many garden visits.

Special Features

- Arboretums
- Asian Garden Styles
- B.C. Garden Shows
- Blossom Safaris
- Botanical Gardens
- Bulb Gardens
- Butterfly Conservatories
- Chinese Classical Garden
- Chinese Tea Gardens
- Cottage Gardens
- Flowers and Canadians
- Garden Tours
- Gardens and Tea
- Haunted Gardens
- Herb Gardens
- Heritage or Settlers' Gardens
- Horticultural Tie-ins
- Japanese Gardens
- Japanese Tea Ceremony
- Language of Flowers
- Manor House Gardens
- Maze Gardens
- Native Plant Gardens
- Parks with Gardens
- Pleasances
- Physick Gardens
- History of B.C. Gardens
- History of Canadian Roses
- History of Glass Palaces
- History of Roses
- History of World Gardens
- Research Gardens
- Rhododendron Gardens
- Rural Gardens
- Special Interest Gardens
- Tea Houses & Tea Gardens
- Undersea Garden
- Victorian Garden Style
- Vineyards and Wineries
- Water Gardens
- Wedding Gardens
- Wheelchair Access
- Wildflower Reserves

Spring flowers in bloom

day's waterwise native plant gardens, B.C.'s abundant show gardens await your exploration.

Today, popular interest in the history of garden trends, both worldwide and regional, is exploding—a natural outgrowth of the movement to conserve worthwhile historic buildings and the environment. In Britain, the popular Garden History Society was founded in 1965 and in America, the Garden Conservancy was established in 1989. The first-ever Museum of Garden History was established in 1977 on the south bank of the River Thames in London to preserve the tombs of the Tradescants; see page 41. Burgeoning interest in B.C. gardens is evidenced by the enthusiastic re-

sponse to gardening programs at VanDusen Botanical Gardens, Vancouver.

In this book, the ever-present links between lush summer gardens and drinking tea

> *"For what is a garden without its roots?"*

are well represented in both the western and Asian traditions. For the ecologically minded, conservation issues from butterflies to healing herbs are yours to explore. If you are a trivia buff, you will love the romance of B.C.'s four

haunted gardens. If you appreciate the bounty of the land, there are wineries to visit and fruit pies to sample. This book will be a lasting remembrance of your visit. This guidebook is a lay person's quick review of garden history and how it affects B.C.'s current horticultural world. It outlines British Columbia's distinctive styles, some of which you may encounter for the first time. Since every garden's location is identified, this book opens the whole beautiful world of British Columbia's public gardens to you. Enjoy!

Clockwise from top left: Statue of Queen Victoria and British Columbia's legislature; Page at Olde England Inn; Hatley Castle; Lawn bowlers and Crystal Garden

Captain G.H. Ogilvie's Luncheon Party on the occasion of the Ladies' Cricket Match, Victoria, ca. 1890.

Greater Victoria Gardens

Why has this city, on the westernmost edge of Canada, nowhere near the Atlantic Ocean, retained such fond attachments to Britain?

A century before Canada's interior was settled, great sailing ships were the primary means of transportation. By the late 1700s, British Naval ships arriving via the southern tip of South America sailed the Pacific West Coast and set up a stopover point on the southern tip of Vancouver Island. This established a British presence that has remained undiminished in over 200 years. Victoria owes the fame of its gardens to an accident of fortunate timing and the invention

By 1845, plants were shipped worldwide in the newly invented Wardian Case. The sealed environment vastly improved plant survival rates.

of a device that allowed plants to survive ocean journeys. In 1842, in London, England, Dr. Nathaniel Bagshaw Ward published a paper entitled "On the Growth of Plants in Closely Glazed Cases." He discovered that a sealed glass case formed a self-sustaining environment for plants. The horticultural

world jumped at the "Wardian Case," and deck-sized greenhouses were immediately put to use on board ships. British commercial interests shipped robust plants among their colonies and plantations. Tea plants moved from China to India; quinine and rubber trees moved around the world. Thanks to this invention, all plants arrived in good condition. The Wardian Case revolutionized living conditions in Britain's colonial settlements. For a time, the British were able to keep the new technology a secret from Americans, who at the time were using ox bladders to transport seedlings.

Also in 1842, the Imperial

British Government instructed Hudson's Bay Company (HBC) employee, James Douglas, to colonize Vancouver Island and thereby prevent further American expansion of the Oregon Territory. Douglas established Fort Victoria and quietly declared British-style rule. Newcomers delighted in the game, good soil and a climate that was stunningly similar to milder regions of England. New colonists, motivated by an unexpected inland gold rush, not only brought their crystal decanters, silver, linen, china and pianos, they were able to send away to England for seedlings, flowers, bulbs and fruit trees. Governor Douglas mentions the innovative "Wardian Case" in his diaries and eagerly anticipates the arrival of his bulbs and roots. Until that time, HBC employees were limited to importing seeds for root vegetables, cabbages and grains; see page 144. The innovative Wardian Case enabled Fort Victoria's residents to import flowers and fruit trees. Residents attempted to enjoy life's gentle pleasures.

Early picnics and catered luncheons were outstanding. Servants with dozens of hampers of food, champagne, wine, brandy, sherry and lemonade would set up "in the country" or at each other's houses. Following a cricket match, up to 40 people would make merry, and perhaps end the day with a candlelight dinner on the deck of a visiting ship. The local "smithie" not only shod horses, he made wrought iron candle centrepieces. By 1868,

the Saanich Peninsula held its first Agricultural Fair. It seems "Victoria," "plants" and "flowers" have long since been mentioned in the same breath.

And elsewhere during the generations from the 1850s to 1880s? The map of western Canada was still marked "Great Wastelands" and the lawless American west was busy defining the "wild" in "Wild West." Victorians continue to recall their founding period with a superior inhaling breath. Sniff.

Annual Flower Count in Victoria

Today, Victoria is alternately known as the "City of Gardens" or "Canada's Best Bloomin' City." Each February, Victorians secretly delight in flaunting their good fortune to Canadians still locked in the icy grip of winter. Since 1976, Victoria's residents have engaged in a tongue-in-cheek ritual called the "Annual Flower Count." During the second and third weeks of February, while most Canadians are counting snowflakes, Victoria's residents emerge from their winter sequestration, calculators in hand, and concentrate on their crocus beds and bulb plantings. They scour boulevards and parks, and peer at the early buds on their flowering fruit trees. Each and every blossom is meticulously counted and the results phoned in to volunteers at Flower Count Mission Control. The grand total is discussed gleefully on call-in radio shows and relayed to thousands of media outlets from North America to Asia. 1997's final count, down from almost 500 million the previous year, was 405,061,185 blooms. The reaction from the rest of Canada ranges from longing

News from Victoria's February Flower Count is often received by the rest of Canada with envious longing.

sighs to Scrooge-like indifference. Of course, Victoria's passionate gardeners are secretly amused. And each February, Canadians are again reminded of a certain Pacific coast "paradise," and its bloomin' spring flowers. For the results of this year's Annual Flower Count, phone Tourism Victoria, (250) 382-2160.

Victorian-Era Garden Style

During the Victorian era, working in the garden was considered morally enriching and virtuous.
Inset: English Victorian-era garden designer Gertrude Jekyll.

Before Queen Victoria's reign (1836-1901), gardens throughout the world were largely the domain of royalty and the upper classes. The contribution of this era to garden style was the popularization of hobby gardening for the masses. Newspapers of the day reported on well funded plant explorers who traveled the world gathering new species. Hybridization programs resulted in hardy plant varieties and practical know-how. Victorian technology made enormous advances: in 1830, the lawn mower was invented; plant propagation and fertilization were standardized; glass greenhouses were improved; the Wardian Case allowed healthy specimens to move around the world. Newly published garden magazines taught common folks how to cultivate flowers and vegetables. Every religious movement of the time extoled the virtues of honest hard work—a philosophy that encouraged the pursuit of hobby gardening.

Miss Gertrude Jekyll (1843-1932), an English garden designer, tirelessly promoted the concept of the garden border. She mixed bedding plants of various heights, explored sequential blooming and matching flower colours. Through her writings, she popularized the simple garden plot for common folks. The "bedding-out" system (planting young seedlings in spring) began to function commercially. New varieties of hardy vegetables for challenging climates improved the kitchen garden. Garden shows, garden tours and garden competitions began everywhere.

Floramania emerged—an indispensable part of courtship among young lovers. Each flower was imbued with meaning and bouquets contained secret messages sent in the "language of flowers." Gentle ladies rendered watercolour paintings of field flowers; some books remain in print today. Flower arranging became a pastime and the commercial florist industry—floral bouquets for special occasions—was born. Even the disadvantaged met with some success selling violets and posies in the streets; think of Eliza Doolittle in the play "My Fair Lady."

Indoors, the glass conservatory became a desirable addition, and home decorating fads included potted palm trees, orchids and tropical plants. Brides chose home weddings to show off their floral decorating skills. Among aristocrats eager to outdo the newly enthusiastic middle classes, the Grand Garden Style emerged. Royal estates were revamped with statues, flower borders, sweeping treed lanes, elaborate fountains, grand outbuildings and arboretums. Many estate grounds opened to the public—most for the first time. The colonial population of Victoria in Canada eagerly embraced each of these garden practices as soon as their resources permitted.

Ann Hathaway's Cottage in Victoria is surrounded by a typical English cottage garden.

Ann Hathaway's Cottage Garden: Victoria

Though aristocrats may have defined the development of garden landscaping, many of the common garden flowers we enjoy today, we owe to common folks—villagers—who found time to nurture a plant they spotted struggling in a ditch.

Long before the Victorian era, common folks enjoyed a hodgepodge around their cottages. A wife might tend a few culinary herbs, but in the outer yard, wildflowers were jumbled with vines, cabbages with clumps of weeds. The lowly cottage garden provided many a sheltered young girl with her first introduction to nature. Though women were not considered fit for horticultural careers, countless generations extracted flower essences, tended herbs and kept nature diaries. When aristocrats' servants threw "weeds" out, commoners snapped them up. Later, these plants became fashionable again—rediscovered in cottagers' gardens. Once-forgotten flowers that later became rich folks' fancies include ranunculas, anemones, hyacinths, pinks, pansies and the once-disdained Hollyhock.

Visitors are invited to enjoy a prime example of a jumbled cottage garden; the jumble is as it should be. Beside it is a full-sized replica of Ann Hathaway's thatched cottage and a charming English Village Square. Afternoon high tea is served in the adjoining Olde English Inn. Reservations for tea are advised; (250) 388-4353. Admission is charged. Wheelchair accessibility is fair.

Location: Olde England Inn & Ann Hathaway's Thatched Cottage, 429 Lampson Street, Victoria.

Ann Hathaway and Shakespeare

A replica of the original Hathaway cottage in Shottery, England.

On November 27, 1582, the 18-year-old William Shakespeare married 28-year-old Ann Hathaway. On May 26, 1583, Ann bore their first daughter, Susanna. In 1585, a set of twins was born, Hamnet and Judith. Hamnet died at the age of eleven in 1596. Not a jot is known about Shakespeare's life between 1585 and 1591. By 1592, he was an actor in London where he was writing successful plays.

Recorded history has not been kind to dear Ann. There is little documentation about her life and we certainly do not know if she ever tended a garden. But we do like to imagine. The original "Ann Hathaway's Cottage," family home of prosperous farmer Richard Hathaway, stands in Shottery, England. Its duplicate stands in Victoria. The kitchen, buttery, bedroom and furniture are consistent with the style of the period. The guides provide a hilarious account of life in Elizabethan England.

Arboretums: Victoria

Ross Bay Cemetery

Location: 1495 Fairfield Road, Victoria.

In the 1840s, the so-called "Rural Cemeteries" movement began in eastern Canada. These "pleasure grounds" were the precursors to Canada's public parks. Cemeteries like Mount Royal in Montreal and Mount Pleasant in Toronto were planted with trees and flower beds, then opened to the public. People were expected to drop by, especially after church on Sundays, and enjoy a leisurely stroll. Victoria's early residents, ever alert to such trends, joined the movement.

Today, Ross Bay is a living museum, a testimony to a time when municipal parks were merely an evolving concept. Over the last 150 years, over 100 varieties of trees have been planted among the graves. Though a graveyard seems an unusual place to visit a garden, this century-old arboretum is part of Canadian history, committed to enhancing the enjoyment of visitors while continuing to provide a dignified memorial for those who have passed on.

The Greater Victoria Regional District periodically gives tree identification tours, and one tour company is dedicated to gravesite tours; phone (250) 598-8870. Admission is free. Wheelchair accessibility is fair; the ground is uneven.

Royal Roads Arboretum

Location: 2050 Sooke Road, Royal Roads University and Hatley Castle, Sooke.

Not always given the credit they deserve, arboretums are collections of diverse trees given space to grow to maturity. When placed among the rolling hills of a great estate such as Hatley Castle, they add an unmistakable aura of charm, nostalgia and beauty.

Established at the turn of the 20th century, and still vital a century later, this arboretum provides visitors with a natural conservation area. The castle's first owner, James Dunsmuir, hired landscape architects Messrs. Brett and Hall from Boston, MA to plan the gardens and surrounding grounds. He instructed them to spare no expense in laying out his estate.

Against the background of a massive stone castle, the mature trees are magnificent today, much as they may have been in the mind's eye of the gardeners who planted them. The story of this arboretum and its castle is found on page 32. In addition to the arboretum, a series of formal gardens including an Italian garden and a Japanese garden are open to the public.

Admission is free; a parking fee is required. The area is wheelchair accessible.

Blossoming Tree Sequence: Victoria

Late January	Early February	Late February	Early March	Late March	April
Weeping Higan Cherry *Single or double pink pendulous clusters; may flower as early as November or December*	**Weeping Higan Cherry** *Single or double pink pendulous clusters; may flower as early as November or December*	**Lindsay Plum** *Almond pink blossoms*	**Purple-Leafed Flowering Plum** *Pale pink buds fading to white blossoms*	**Double Pink Higan Cherry (Atsumori Cherry)** *Very deep pink blossoms, double flowers*	**Kanzan Cherry** *Rose pink blossoms, double flowers*
		Double Purple-Leafed Plum *Double pink blossoms, purple leaves*	**Double Purple-Leafed Plum** *Double pink blossoms, purple leaves*	**Magnolia** *White with pink-edged blossoms*	**Ukon Cherry** *White to light pink blossoms*
			Fukuban Cherry *Dark purple buds become semi-double dusty rose blossoms*	**Yoshino Cherry** *White to pinkish blossoms*	**Crabapples** *White to pink blossoms*
				Sargent Cherry *White blossoms*	**Paul's Scarlet Double Hawthorne** *Deep pink blossoms*
					Western Flowering Dogwood *Off-white Blossoms*

Blossoming Tree Safari: Victoria

Blossoming trees are the harbingers of spring, and Victoria boasts many streets lined with row upon row of white or pink blossoms. Flowering trees burst into bloom before they send out their leaves; and after showers of fading flowers flutter to the ground, leaves quickly appear. In addition to the flowering fruit trees listed here, magnolias are especially beautiful in mid-April.

Victoria Tourism and the Victoria Parks Department both provide specific street location lists where hundreds of flowering trees line Victoria's boulevards. Phone (250) 361-9733 for a free location list.

B.C. Native Plant Gardens: Greater Victoria

Since the time of the first settlers, B.C. residents have extoled the province's natural botanical beauty and ideal climate. By contrast, its gardeners have filled their pots with imported species. The elements that distinguish B.C. from the rest of Canada—a year-round growing climate and bountiful horticultural diversity—make it relatively easy to experiment with horticultural styles. As a result, B.C. gardeners are adept at growing non-indigenous plants; see page 156.

Today, a new movement is gaining momentum. Forward-looking people who are ecologically aware are working hard to increase home gardeners' and municipalities' appreciation for native vegetation. In most cases, this vegetation is easier to grow, more winter hardy and requires less water than imported plant species. Several organizations now spread the message. Some B.C. municipalities have adopted a native-plant-only policy. The challenge of this approach is public perception: indigenous plant species are

Native plants for local gardens and for municipal landscaping are a growing trend.

considered common, dreary looking or boring. When one is surrounded with thousands of miles of abundant natural vegetation, the eye longs for the vibrancy of imported flowers. "The challenge for garden designers at present," says David C. Streatfield, prominent American landscape designer, "will be to develop a new tradition based on sound ecological principles that can also refresh and uplift the spirit." Check B.C.'s native plant experiments out for yourself. Admission is free.

Indigenous Plants Beneficial to Wildlife

Shrubs & bushes	Saskatoon berries, beaked hazelnut, salal, Indian plum, wild gooseberry, thimbleberry, salmonberry, flowering red currant
Trees	paper birch, yellow cedar, black cottonwood, Pacific crab apple, cascara
Ground covers	kinnikinnick, bunchberry, woodland strawberry, twinflower, Oregon grape
Perennials	yarrow, wild ginger, Siberian miner's lettuce, Hooker's fairybell, fireweed
Ferns	maidenhair, lady, deer, parsley, oak, licorice

B.C. Native Plant Gardens: Victoria and Saanich

Victoria Compost Demonstration Garden & Water Conservation Garden	1923 Fernwood Road, Victoria	(250) 386-9676
Native Plant Garden; A Project of Friends of the Government House Garden Society	Government House, 1401 Rockland Avenue; native gardens off-limits except by arrangement	(250) 356-5139 Phone ahead to arrange viewing.
Native Plant Garden; specimens from all B.C. regions	Royal British Columbia Museum; 675 Belleville	(250) 387-3701
Swan Lake Christmas Hill Nature Sanctuary & Society, Native Plant Garden	3873 Swan Lake Road, off McKenzie Avenue, near Highway 17, Saanich	(250) 479-0211

Wild Camas Lilies

Legendary Irish-born artist Paul Kane made an early odyssey to the Pacific coast and Vancouver Island in the 1850s. He wrote: "Fort Victoria stands upon the banks of an inlet… its Indian name is the Esquimelt or place for gathering Camas, great quantities of that vegetable being found in the neighbourhood." Early white settlers reported favourably on the tastiness of camas pie, said to resemble a baked pear pie. However, David Douglas, an early plant gatherer traveling through the area in 1839 reported: "assuredly they produce flatulence, when in the Indian hut I was almost blown out by strength of wind."

Camas lily blooms in May and grows at Beacon Hill, Playfair Park and in the Native Plant Garden on the grounds of the Royal British Columbia Museum.

Location: Camas lily blooms in May and grows at Beacon Hill, Playfair Park and in the Native Plant Garden.

Native people once harvested great quantities of wild Camas bulbs, mashed them slightly, compressed them into bricks, and baked up to 50 kg (100 pounds) in underground stone-heated pit ovens. Called *quawmash,* the resulting foodstuff was sweet, nourishing and tasty.

In 1806, while traveling through Washington state, Meriwether Lewis of America's famed Lewis and Clark Expedition compared the colour of Camas blooms to "lakes of clear fine water, so complete in this deseption [sic] that on first sight I could have sworn it was water."

Victoria's Hanging Baskets

Since 1937, Victoria's hanging baskets have been the hallmark of this west coast city. More than 1,000 living bouquets of geraniums, lobelia, marigolds, schizanthus, petunias, nepeta, viscaria, Rose-of-heaven and other flowers hang from old-fashioned light standards.

Seeds for the famous baskets are planted in December in Beacon Hill Park's greenhouses. Seedlings are placed in flats until it's time to transplant them into lined wire baskets. Sphagnum

moss was used for many years, but recently, a new material de-

veloped in British Columbia from organic wood waste has proven effective.

Over the years, different floral combinations were tested for colour, compactness, and above all, durability. Today, the 25 flower-per-basket combinations are well-established.

The window boxes decorating City Hall and the planters stationed about the Inner Harbour are also creations of Victoria Parks Department horticulturists.

Sequestered within the grand garden complex, Jenny Butchart kept her own private garden. Here she could avoid the crowds and have tea with her friends. Today, her private garden remains exactly as she created it.

The Butchart Gardens: Victoria

*I*n 1888, in Owen Sound, Ontario, a former dry goods merchant became interested in the manufacture of Portland Cement. By the turn of the century, Mr. Robert Pim Butchart had become a successful cement manufacturer but as eastern competition grew, his attention was drawn to rich deposits of limestone and clay in the far west of Vancouver Island. In 1904, he relocated his family, established a home, and built a new cement factory at Tod Inlet.

As Mr. Butchart's enterprise exhausted the limestone quarry near their home, his innovative wife, Jenny, conceived an unprecedented plan.

Mrs. Jenny Butchart

She would refurbish the bleak pit and turn it into a splendid garden. From the very start, she had a vision, "I vowed that if I ever had a garden, less fortunate people than myself should have the privilege of enjoying it." With that, she requisitioned horses and carts to bring in loads of topsoil. Little by little, without a formal plan, a garden emerged where an ugly scar had been. She planted Lombardy poplars to screen off the manufacturing plant and then, dangling from the quarry cliffs in a bosun's chair, she herself stuffed ivy into the rocky crevices. With the help of a landscape expert to advise her on drainage and workers from her husband's factory, she organized her resources to realize her flowering dream.

By 1906, garden-building-fever was in full swing. Jenny engaged landscape artist

Left: Sunken Garden: "One's senses are almost intoxicated into the belief that it is not real at all, but just a marvelous vision that must presently vanish." —Nellie DeBertrand Lugrin, writer, on Butchart's Sunken Garden, 1931

Isaboru Kishida to design a seaside Japanese Garden in 1928. Reflecting on the sights she and her husband gleaned during their world travels, she then went on to create a symmetrical Italian Garden. Word of Mrs. Butchart's gardening marvels spread quickly. By 1915, tea was served to the 18,000 people a year who dropped by to visit. And by 1929, when she engaged Mr. Butler Sturtevant of Seattle to design the Rose Garden, more than 50,000 people a year came to see her magical creation. In a gracious gesture toward their visitors, the hospitable Butcharts christened their garden-estate *Benvenuto*, the Italian word for "welcome." And neither would allow a single "Do Not ..." sign on the property. Finally, during the war in 1941, the Butcharts were forced to rescind their complimentary policy, and began charging 25¢ admission to maintain the grounds.

As their lives drew to a close, the Butcharts were asked to relate their life story. "Once there was a pretty little girl who married a man and lived happily ever after," was all they would volunteer.

The Gardens remain the property of the Butchart family. From 1938 to 1997 Mr. Robert Ian Ross, grandson of the Butcharts, philanthropist and long-time friend of the University of Victoria and his wife, Ann-Lee, operated the Gardens.

The Butchart Gardens celebrates its 100th anniversary in 2004.

A Summer's Day at The Butchart Gardens

The Butchart Gardens open at 9 a.m. daily. Tour bus groups, individuals, families and groups immediately begin to arrive. Well prepared for most contingencies, The Gardens provides umbrellas, wheelchairs and comforting amenities to alleviate challenging situations.

However, during the busy spring and summer season, the public areas can be crowded by noon. Plan on at least $10 per person for a light lunch.

An alternative strategy is to plan your visit for late afternoon. If you arrive around 3 p.m. you can enjoy the flowers by daylight, stop for refreshments, enjoy the live entertainment and stroll in the gardens again after the lights are turned on. Musicians, buskers and magicians perform often.

A Summer's Night at The Butchart Gardens

"Night Illuminations" or garden lightup begins late in the afternoon and by the time the sun goes down between June 15 and September 15, The Butchart Gardens and Ross Fountain are bathed in fairyland colours. Restaurants stay open in the evenings. Every Saturday in July and August, the evening's excitement includes fireworks—a sparkling ending to a long summer day. Check for times and

dates. On fireworks nights, admission gates close when the parking lots are full, so come early in the afternoon. Alternately, on some summer evenings, a group of theatrical players presents a glittery, lighthearted evening stage show on the Concert Lawn Stage; phone ahead for performance times.

Sunny morning *Sunny afternoon* *Overcast day* *Early evening*

A Photographer's Day and Night at The Butchart Gardens

On overcast or rainy days, the Sunken Garden makes a particularly good photography subject with few shadows. On sunny days, the garden looks wonderful, but the camera sees deep black shadows in the morning and afternoon. For the best photos, time your visit for overcast days. When photographing the Sunken Garden look up to your right and note the wooden teahouse. It is designed to provide a better view of the quarry pit. Take advantage of this special service.

Night photography, when the coloured lights bathe the gardens in primary tones, can be particularly rewarding. When taking time exposures of the Sunken Gardens at night, do not impede the flow of visitors entering the quarry. Because moving people leave streaks across your time-exposed photographs, wait patiently to capture a 30-second stretch without pedestrians.

The Butchart Boar

In 1620, Italian sculptor Pietro Tacca cast a bronze figure imitating the marble boar, "Cinghiale," now on display at Uffizi Gallery in Florence. Art authorities have suggested that the original marble boar was once part of a larger grouping, possibly a hunting scene. The animal's position suggests neither repose nor attack. Rather, it seems startled, perhaps by the sound of a hunting horn. Tacca's bronze casting, called "Porcellino," is well loved and sits on the south side of the Straw Market in Florence. For generations his long nose has been affectionately burnished to bring good luck. However, Tacca modified the design of the original, adding a base with a small pool, frogs, snakes and a turtle.

Mr. and Mrs. Ross acquired a rare copy of Porcellino on a trip to Italy. Today, its well-rubbed bronze nose attests to its popularity in The Butchart Gardens. The Butchart statue has been dubbed "Tacca" in honour of its creator.

Butchart's Theme Gardens and Facilities

Best of Show Greenhouse
Begonia Bower
Blue Poppy Cafeteria
Coffee Bar and Soda Fountain
Concert Lawn
Dining Room
Fireworks Staging Area
Three Sturgeons Fountain
Italian Garden
Japanese Garden
Ocean Lookout
Plant Identification Centre
Rose Garden,
Ross Fountain
Seed and Gift Store
Star Pond and Fountain
Sunken Garden

Through the Year at The Butchart Gardens

Early spring

Though seasonal changes alter the face of The Butchart Gardens, they are always interesting.

In winter, the bare bones of the gardens anticipate things to come. Gentle variances of texture and colour distinguish broadleaf evergreens and conifers, berry trees and shrubs. Hints of spring arrive with early pansies and English daisies, Polyanthus and primroses. Bright red holly berries and pink heather are a welcome burst of colour on a gray winter day.

Against a backdrop of blossoming trees and shrubs—forsythia, jasmine, pieris and flowering Japanese cherries—the early March crocus heralds the arrival of wallflowers. The last week of March is the best time to see hyacinths and daffodils. In April, more than 100,000 bulbs open. Along with pastel narcissi, daffodils, flowering plums, crabapples and some 30 species of flowering shrubs. Rhododendrons and azaleas start to show, and the native Western flowering dogwood begins the first of its two flowering cycles.

In mid- to late April, tulips pop up in a palette of colours, followed by flowering rhododendrons, azaleas and early perennials. Siberian wallflowers and forget-me-nots are both colourful and fragrant, and the rare handkerchief or dove tree (*Davidia involucrata*) is at its peak. Gloriously coloured Cinerarias bloom at this time and hanging baskets overflow with Schizanthus.

In June, the azaleas and late rhododendrons are at their best. Columbine, Delphiniums and in more shaded places, the rare Himalayan blue poppy join Nemesia, tuberous begonias, stocks, poppies and sweet William. Weigela, Deutzia and beauty bush are also in full bloom. The Rose Garden boasts spectacular

Late summer

Through the Year at The Butchart Gardens

Early summer

colours during the last two weeks of June, and for many visitors, this is the star attraction.

During the months of July and August, ever-changing beds of annuals supply non-stop colour. Perennials are at their peak and roses in all different forms—climbing, rambling and standard—continue to bloom. The Sunken Garden sports full-grown well-groomed beds, the envy of every home gardener. The hanging baskets reestablish their reputation at this time, and St. John's wort, Godetia, Cosmos, angel's trumpet, and carnations all compete for attention.

In September, displays of tuberous begonias and dahlias reach their zenith. In the perennial borders, towering shocks of red, gold and blue Lychnis, Solidago and fall asters compensate for the shortening days. Hydrangeas and fuchsias prolong summer's glory.

The fall colours peak in October with flaming red and russet Japanese maples. Magnificent arbutus trees and copper beech add more colour to the autumnal scene. The dahlias maintain their splendour until the first frosts come, as do many varieties of Chrysanthemums. It is once

again time to plant the bulbs for spring. Above the sleeping bulbs in freshly tilled beds, pansies and daisies await the spring.

Replacing the autumn colours of November come sparkling Christmas lights which set the evenings aglow from December 1 to January 6. Many families come to visit The Butchart Gardens at Christmas time, when the berries join the holly, carolers and festive entertainment to add to the holiday atmosphere. The Butchart Gardens delight visitors every month of the year.

Winter

Flowers are displayed both indoors and out at The Butchart Gardens

Information: The Butchart Gardens

Size	20 ha (50 acres)
Time allotment	3 to 5 hours
Open	9:00 a.m. to variable closing; in winter at 4 p.m.; in summer from 7 p.m. to 9 p.m. Note: Come early for special events. Admission gates close when the parking lots are full.
Year round	Yes
Best seasons	Late spring, summer, autumn
Sub-gardens	Sunken Garden, Ross Fountain, Rose Garden, Begonia Bower, Concert Lawn, Star Pond, Italian Garden, Japanese Garden, Show Greenhouse
Additional facilities	Restaurants: Coffee Bar, Soda Fountain, Blue Poppy Cafeteria, Seed & Gift Store, Plant Identification Centre, The Dining Room. Note: Admission to the gardens is required for restaurant access.
Additional services	Loaner umbrellas, cameras, wheelchairs, baby push-carts, luggage storage, postage stamp sales
Events	Night Illuminations, Saturday summer fireworks, Butchart buskers, a stage show, Christmas time entertainment
Admission charged	Yes, at the time of this writing, it is approximately $15 per person
Wheelchair access	Yes, mostly accessible
Guided tours	No. However, a garden map is available in 18 languages.
Telephone	Recording (250)652-5256; business (250) 652-4422; fine dining reservations (250) 652-8222; fax (250)652-3883 E-mail: email@butchartgardens.b.c.ca
Location	1) Located on Vancouver Island, north of the city of Victoria on the Saanich Peninsula; it is 21 km (13 miles) north of Victoria or 20 km (12.5 miles) south of the Vancouver-Victoria ferry terminal at Swartz Bay. Vancouver Island is serviced year-round by tour bus companies, public transit buses, frequent daily ferry sailings and airline flights. 2) If you are in Victoria (city), take Blanchard Street North. This becomes Pat Bay Highway; turn left (west) onto Keating X Road. 3) Alternately, if you are arriving by ferry at Swartz Bay, you may want to go to the gardens before proceeding to Victoria (city). Follow Highway 17 to Keating X Road, turn west. 4) Additionally, you can access the Gardens by yacht or by float plane.
Nearby attractions	Victoria Butterfly Gardens

As night falls, the crowd thins out and the garden dazzles anew.

Butchart's Japanese Garden

When *spring comes From the tip of every branch Flowers will bloom, But the crimson leaves of, Last year, the little ones, Will never again return.*
—Ryokan Taigu in *Three Zen Masters*, 1993

Evoking her travels around the world, Mrs. Butchart engaged landscape artist Isaboru Kishida in 1906 to design a seaside Japanese garden. Working on a relatively steep side of the site, he designed a lush, green area with sago palms, Japanese black pines, cut-leaf red maple, heavenly bamboo, camellias, azaleas and ajuga. Japanese landscape garden skills are passed down through generations and Kishida's expertise served him well. The Butcharts' grandson, Ian Ross, later revisited this part of the garden and

Bridge and The Japanese Garden

modified it to better reflect its Asian roots. The Stroll-style garden is designed to harmonize with the natural landforms. Its elements, from the lush green hillside to the streams, ponds, and small waterfall are carefully arranged to create space for quiet meditation. An arched bridge, tumbling waterfall, bamboo fences, streams and ponds soothe the senses. Every rock is positioned to expose patterns of lichen and mosses, to create a symbolic grouping, or to guide tumbling waters. At night, this area of the garden is a must-see; its distinctive shapes are particularly striking under coloured lights. For more information on Japanese garden style, see page 82.

What Makes The Butchart Gardens So Popular?

A poet, a gardener, a tourist, a psychologist and a marketing expert ought to discuss this topic. It is true that Victoria has been associated with flowers since its founding. And word is bound to get around about any tourist attraction that manages to survive for almost 100 years. Part of its appeal was Mrs. Butchart's hospitality, but other wealthy patrons have built more perfect gardens that attracted far less attention. Perhaps the pent-up aesthetic needs of early settlers, unexpectedly hungry for the gentle beauties of their homelands is the reason. But why has its popularity endured for generations?

One analysis of The Butchart Gardens' popularity is derived from the conversations of visitors. Many seem compelled to reflect on their own garden patches back home: "Now this is exactly what I want to do with that little open strip… you know.. the one beside the shed…."

Is this the key to Butchart's appeal? Somehow, Jenny's largely untutored determination to transform an ugly industrial quarry into a beautiful garden satisfies a secret longing in many people. Whatever our personal gardening dreams may be, The Butchart Gardens' unpretentious aesthetics have been acclaimed since the moment of their inception. Mrs. Butchart somehow makes it look easy.

Craigflower's Heritage Gardens: Victoria

Three well researched settler's gardens are located at Craigflower Farmhouse, ca. 1853. To grow the settler-style gardens here, original plants on site were revived, authentic seeds were imported from England's Wellsburn Genetic Seedbanks, and old varieties were gathered from early European settlement sites around the province.

From Craigflower Farm's meticulous account records, we can determine the names of the original plants.

The children's garden is planted according to the diaries of the first Governor's daughter. From the wilds, Martha collected yarrow, wild ginger, Hooker's fairybell and fireweed. To this she added ferns: maidenhair, lady, deer, parsley, oak and licorice. She also grew imported red English daisies.

Craigflower Farmhouse

The Hudson's Bay Company kitchen garden is planted in raised beds. While HBC employees were encouraged to grow turnips, cabbages and some grains, they managed to add imported daisies, daylilies, goldenrods, and fall asters.

The heirloom orchard is planted with old semi-dwarf varieties of apples, plum, quince and a cherry tree. One variety dating to the 1700s, a dessert apple from France, is called "Lady."

Unlike visits to flashy show gardens, trips to heritage gardens are educational. The more you know about the sites, the more interesting they become. There is an admission fee to visit Craigflower Farmhouse; its heritage gardens are free. The area is mostly wheelchair accessible.

Location: Admirals Road and Craigflower Road, Highway 1A, Victoria.

Dr. Helmcken's Healing Garden

Dr. Helmcken, Fort Victoria's first doctor, arrived in 1850. His house, still in its original location, now displays his antique medical instruments. Outside his home, herbs from his medicinal Physick Garden are grown each year. During his training at Guys Hospital, London, Dr. Helmcken learned to grow Digitalis, lavender, comfrey, chamomile and other therapeutic plants for his patients. Without growing his own therapeutic herbs, he would have had little to prescribe. His letters from the 1850s mention the red English daisies he imported at the exorbitant price of $1

Helmcken House and its "Physick Garden"

English daisies

each to plant over his daughters' graves. Admission to the house is charged; the small planted area is free. The area is wheelchair accessible.

Location: Helmcken House, east of the Royal British Columbia Museum next to 675 Belleville Street.

Heritage Gardens in British Columbia

After the back-breaking work of clearing the land, early settlers delighted in growing a few frivolous flowers.

Costumed animator at Burnaby Village Museum.

"**We [the government** of British Columbia] invest a lot in creating heritage gardens, but I'm not sure visitors always appreciate their significance," says Jennifer Iredale, Curator and Content Provider of the Heritage Branch. "These recreated settler's gardens are authentic and rare. Exactly like British Columbia's earliest residents, we still go to England and their genetic seed banks to import seeds."

Today in B.C., several heritage gardens are carefully researched and designed to reflect vegetation from a particular time period. Among B.C. residents, interest in Colonists or settlers gardens is keen. Rare old genetic seed stock exchanges are held annually both in Victoria and Vancouver. B.C. Heritage Attractions, a provincial government body, maintains several well-researched gardens.

Despite the effort settlers exerted in building homesteads, starting kitchen gardens, fruit orchards, and setting up the infrastructure for a new society, pioneer women found time to coax a few flowers to life to serve as fond reminders of home.

Recreated Heritage Gardens in British Columbia

Burnaby Village Museum, 1900s	Kitchen garden, borders	Burnaby
Carr House, 1920s	Homemaker's garden	Victoria
Craigflower Farm, 1850s	Kitchen garden, heirloom orchard, children's garden	Victoria
Fort Steele Heritage Site, 1890s	Chinese kitchen garden, early grasses, settlers' gardens, army garden, Victorian-era gardens	Cranbrook
Guisachan House garden, 1920s	Edwardian-era garden	Kelowna
Helmcken House, 1860s	Old physick garden	Victoria
Kilby Store Heritage Site, 1920s	Roominghouse garden	Agassiz
Point Ellice, 1880s	Victorian-era ornamental and kitchen gardens	Victoria
Stewart Farm, 1900	Kitchen garden, flower garden	Surrey
The Grist Mill Heritage Site, 1860-1940	HBC garden, old wheat varieties, rare apples, settler's gardens, heritage orchard	Keremeos

A Brief History of Glass Palaces

• By 10 AD, ancient Romans use steam-heated greenhouses to cultivate roses.

• During the 1600s, British and French aristocrats grow citrus fruit in "orangeries." Poor ventilation kills many plants.

• In 1742, young Lord Petre of Essex, England dies, leaving a quarter million exotic trees to wither in his glass "Stove" House.

Kew Gardens Palm House, 1848

• In 1818, the wrought iron process is industrialized. In 1833, sheet glass up to 1.8 m (6 feet) in length is produced.

• In 1840, Joseph Paxton, gardener for Chatworth's Duke of Devonshire, constructs a Great Stove Conservatory. It is 83 m long, 20 m high. In 1919, Chatsworth's Ninth Duke orders dynamite and blows it up.

• In 1842, Nathaniel Bagshaw Ward introduces the idea for enclosing plants in sealed glass cases.

• In 1848, Kew Gardens builds a glass "Palm House."

• In 1850, Prince Albert decides to mount the world's greatest-ever Exhibition. A great "Crystal Palace" is conceived.

• From the 233 designs submitted, Joseph Paxton's wins. He sketches his design on blotting paper, claiming his ideas emulate "the veins of a water lily."

Crystal Palace, 1851

• The 1851 "Great Exhibition of the Works of All Nations" is a resounding success. Its landmark Crystal Palace covers 7.6 ha (19 acres), has 293,655 panes of coloured glass, 330 huge iron columns, 39 km (24 miles) of gutters and the largest roof ever made to date.

Victorian-era Conservatory, 1880s

Victoria's Crystal Garden, 1925

• In 1853, New York stages its own Worlds Fair, centered by the NY Crystal Palace Exposition.

• The Victorian world goes wild for glass buildings. Home owners add conservatories. Great hotels from Singapore to London build central "palm courts."

• In 1879 in Rio de Janeiro State, a great Palácio-de-Cristal is built.

• The French response to the "Crystal Palace phenomenon" is the centrepiece of their 1889 World Exposition: the Eiffel Tower. The British sniff, "a glass palace, without the glass."

• At the 1893 Chicago World Exposition, 120 carloads of glass, enough to cover 12 ha (29 acres), are used for the roofs.

• In 1914, an elliptical glass-roofed Tea Garden opens atop the elegant Hotel Vancouver. Its innovative glass roof panels are praised by B.C.'s *Engineering Record*.

• In 1925, Crystal Garden is built in Victoria to house the British Empire's largest salt water swimming pool. It includes ballrooms and Tea Gardens.

• In 1939, at the second New York World Exposition, Mr. Walt Disney claims he conceived the idea for "Disneyland" while viewing the glass houses of "Futurama."

Crystal Garden houses tropical plants, vari- macaws, ical birds, and tiny onkeys.

Crystal Garden: Victoria

It was natural for the city of Victoria to want its own great glass palace. Designed by renowned Edwardian-era architects, F. Ratten-bury and P.L. James, the Crystal Garden was constructed in 1925. Its expansive glass roof enclosed the largest saltwater pool in the British Empire.

While youngsters learned to swim, the rest of the family used its ballrooms, a tea-room and a prom-enade conservatory. Families would arrange for their fashionably attired daughters to meet proper young men under the watchful eyes of their parents.

In 1971, with upkeep costs soaring and families no longer interested in "afternoon tea dances," the costly pool and ballrooms were replaced. Today, it is an indoor conservatory displaying tropical plants, butterflies, miniature monkeys and endangered species of birds. Admission is charged. The area is wheelchair accessible.

Location: 713 Douglas Street, Victoria, behind the Empress Hotel.

Camellias and Tea

Over a thousand years ago in China, the *Camellia japonica* was highly prized. In approximately 1700, the first live specimens arrived in England. By 1800, the "Japanese rose" was lovingly grown in estate "stove" houses. Because it was difficult to care for, it gradually fell out of favour. Then in 1917, in Yunnan province, China George Forrest collected new varieties which became hardy Camellias for northern climes.

Camellia's close cousin, the *Camellia sinensis*, is known more commonly as the tea plant. Its identity and growing habits were closely guarded secrets. In 1843, England's Robert Fortune (1812-1880) made the first of four journeys to China. Disguised as a local, he stole the secrets of cultivating tea, and eventually sent 24,000 tea plants and 17,000 germinated seedlings to northern India via

Camellia japonica

the Wardian Case. Never before had so many Chinese plants survived transportation.

A wild tea plant can become a tree reaching 30 m (100 feet) in height. Monkeys were once trained to pick the leaves and throw them down. Today, for easy plucking, *C. sinensis* is kept to a height of about one m (3 feet). Common tea leaf blends come from India, Sri Lanka, Kenya, Malawi, Indonesia and China, though a total of 1,500 different tea varieties are grown in 25 countries. Tea grows well in acidic soil and a warm climate with at least 1,250 mm (50 inches) of rain each year. The climate, altitude, type of soil, method of processing and the way the finished mixture is blended affects the flavour. Green teas are unoxidized or unfermented; black tea is made by fermenting the leaves.

Unfortunately, *Camellia sinensis* bushes are not as attractive as their ornamental cousins and are never grown in public gardens. Nonetheless, there seems to be a natural affinity between gardens, flowers, Camellias and tea time, all of which evoke thoughts of Victoria.

Suzhou And Victoria: Twin Garden Cities

The ancient city of Suzhou in China, known as "the City of Gardens" and Victoria, known as "the Garden City," are said to share certain common traits.

Both are exceptionally scenic cities. Suzhou is renowned for its whitewashed houses, willow-lined avenues, temples and bridges, while Victoria is known for its spring blossoms, garden-lined avenues, English churches and baby blue bridge. Suzhou, like Venice, is criss-crossed with small canals; Victoria rests on the seashore. Both cities are tranquil retirement centres and tourist meccas. Because of these similarities and in the spirit of international friendship, the two cities were officially twinned in 1980. In nearby Vancouver, the same Suzhou connections inspired the Chinese

community to build Dr. Sun-Yet Sen Classical Chinese Gardens, a model of a Ming dynasty Scholar's Garden; see page 76.

Suzhou has a vibrant garden history. During the Five Dynasties period from 907 to 960, the peaceful Wu and Yue kingdoms became the richest provinces in China. The area's ruler, Qian Liu, led the local gentry in building villa gardens. Because of its genial climate, excellent canal system and lovely garden stones, many wealthy statesmen with political appointments sought to retire in Suzhou; see pages 74 and 129. Later, during the Yuan period from 1279 to 1368, another lot of officials retired to Suzhou, built grand retirement houses and attached beautiful high-walled Chinese gardens. Suzhou was not only wealthy, it became a centre of gardening art.

In western circles today, Suzhou gardens are referred to as "Chinese Classical Gardens." Although many were destroyed during the 1851 Taiping Revolution, hundreds more were built during the 1950s. Today, nine Suzhou gardens are open to

the public. Their beauty is reflected in an old saying: "Above is Heaven, (just) below are Hangzhou and Suzhou."

On October 22, 1980, Mayor Tindall of Victoria and Pan Linru, Vice-Chairman of Suzhou Municipal Revolutionary Committee signed a proclamation declaring Victoria and Suzhou "sister cities." As a token of celebration, the City of Victoria gave its sister city 5,000 daffodil bulbs, two blue light standards and a Native totem pole. The bulbs were planted and the light standards and totem pole installed in the Eastern Garden in Suzhou.

In return, the City of Suzhou gave Victoria a pair of chimeras—lions with dragon-like personalities—a Chinese painting and a piece of reversible Suzhou embroidery. Victoria placed the stone chimeras in front of the Gate of Harmonious Interest at the entry to Victoria's Chinatown. It is said that the mythical twin chimeras will come alive the day an honest politician passes between them. No problem so far.

Thousands of bulbs grace the gardens in spring and in summer the glass Gazebo is used for outdoor entertaining.

Government House Gardens: Victoria

Government House in the Rockland district is the residence of the Lieutenant-Governor, the provincial representative of the Queen. When a member of the royal family is in Victoria, this is where they reside. Surrounded by expansive grounds and manicured gardens, this vice-regal mansion rivals the legendary Rideau Hall in Ottawa. Although the great stone house is closed to the public, nearly 4 ha (10 acres) of mixed gardens are open during daylight hours.

Dr. David Lam, recent Lieutenant-Governor, revamped several subgardens and added a small Asian-style garden. On lower ground are Mrs. Rogers' Rose Garden, and a second Victorian Rose Garden. The Duck Pond is a sedate place to stop awhile

Admission is free. The area is wheelchair accessible. There are no public washrooms.

Location: 1401 Rockland Avenue, Victoria.

Garry Oak

Nicknamed the "broccoli tree" for its distinctive silhouette, the Garry Oak is Victoria's signature tree. The *Quercus garryana* grows on relatively dry, rocky slopes and bluffs. Also known as the Oregon White Oak, its deeply lobed, shiny green leaves deteriorate as summer progresses. Its bitter acorns were once soaked, leached and eaten by the Salish people of the Puget Sound region. Its bark was one of the ingredients in "Saanich four-barks," a native medicine said to combat tuberculosis and other ailments. Garry Oaks are abundant in Beacon Hill Park and throughout Victoria.

Taken on one of the rare occasions James Dunsmuir was not aboard his yacht, this archival photo shows the coal baron relaxing with his family. Below: James Dunsmuir

Hatley Castle Park Gardens: Sooke

Hatley Park Castle, the 1908 Edwardian estate, and its gardens were born of the dogged determination of coal baron James Dunsmuir. Born at Fort Rupert, B.C. on July 8, 1851, he was the oldest son a Scots miner who sought coal on "Vancouver's" Island. It was not until 1869, when James was 18 years old, that his father finally discovered a rich seam near Nanaimo. After raising sufficient capital, his father started his mining operations. James worked through the ranks, and upon becoming manager he raised the daily coal output from 30 to 1,500 tons. After his father's death in 1889, James devoted himself to his collieries at Wellington and Cumberland, and sold coal to the Americans in San Francisco and to the Royal Navy at Esquimalt.

The coal business eventually lead James into politics. He was elected to the Legislature in 1898 and became premier of the province in 1900. Having little taste for public service, and enduring public humiliation in the form of a lawsuit with his mother over the division of his father's estate, he resigned prematurely in 1902. He later served as Provincial Lieutenant Governor.

In 1908, James purchased 344 ha (850 acres) of land and, having amassed a fortune, began to build his retirement mecca. "Money doesn't matter, just build what I want," was his oft-quoted phrase. Architect Samuel Maclure designed the "Castle" with a 27 m (82 foot) turret, and Messrs. Brett and Hall, landscape artists from Boston, planned the lavish gardens and arboretum. Saturna Island and Valdez Island sandstone was quarried for the building's

outer walls and the lavish interior appointments included oak and rosewood paneling, baronial fireplaces, teak floors, and hand-crafted lighting fixtures. The stone wall surrounding the estate cost over $75,000; the glass conservatory, was once filled with brilliant white orchids imported from India, complementing a large banana tree growing under the central dome. The separate greenhouses were filled with ferns, flowers, vegetables, peach trees and palm trees. The boiler keeping the plants warm burned 100 tons of coal and 200 cords of wood a year. This enabled servants to fill the house with cut flowers year-round and to provide the family with a never-ending supply of fresh hothouse vegetables. The lands were interlaced with 10 km (6 miles) of roads and over one hundred men were employed to maintain the gardens.

The $4 million Castle and its grounds were completed in 1908, and the Dunsmuir family quickly took up residence. Early in 1910, James sold his businesses for $11 million. He then retired to his estate, his gardens and his yacht, *Delora*, to hunt, fish and golf. After his death in 1920, his wife Laura and daughter Eleanor remained at the castle.

In November 1940, the Dominion Government purchased the estate at the bargain price of $75,000—the price Dunsmuir paid to build the exterior wall alone. In December of the same year the estate became the HMCS Royal Roads, an Officer Training Establishment, the first of several military training

Left: Hatley Castle's Italian Garden

institutes. On February 22,1994, an ever-downsizing military announced that Royal Roads Military College would close. With strong public support, the Province of British Columbia and the federal government established Royal Roads Military College, which became Royal Roads University. On March 17, 1996, at the recommendation of the Historic Sites and Monuments Board of Canada, Hatley Park received National Historic Site designation.

Fortunately, the gardens were maintained since their original construction. Consisting of the Neptune Steps, the Italian Gardens, the Japanese Garden and Lake, the Rose Garden and the Upper and Lower Lakes, the gardens are open at no charge to the public.

The Conservatory no longer exists. Its foundations are still visible. The greenhouses are used extensively. They contain a 90-year-old grape vine—a true heirloom plant. It was grown from cuttings of the "Hamburg," a

According to Japanese philosopher Mokichi Okada, the bridge in a Japanese Garden represents the indivisibility of the physical and the spiritual. The physical plane is the actual bridge and the spiritual plane is its reflection in the water.

famous black grape vine planted in 1769, and is still an attraction at Hampton Court Palace Gardens in England.

Upon entering the grounds, visitors encounter a statue of the mythical sea god, Neptune (Poseidon). The Italian Gardens are behind the gates, next to the castle. The Central Pavilion, flanked by columns, terminates in vine-covered gazebos. Completing the formal composition are stone benches, floral urns and marble pedestals and marble statues of Pomona, Ceres, Flora and Hebe. Clipped evergreens and parterres make the area a popular spot for

"Money doesn't matter, just build what I want."

— James Dunsmuir

Information: Hatley Castle

Type	Hatley Castle Park is a public garden attached to the Royal Roads University.
Size	252 ha (625 acres)
Time allotment	1 to 2 hours
Open	During daylight hours
Year round	Yes
Best seasons	Late spring, summer, autumn
Sub-gardens	Italian garden, Japanese garden, rose garden, Neptune Steps, Middle Lake
Additional facilities	There are public washrooms; access to the buildings is restricted.
Events	Not applicable
Admission charged	Free to view the gardens; parking fees on the grounds are mandatory.
Wheelchair access	Grounds are mostly accessible. There are public washrooms.
Guided tours	Castle tours take place periodically in summer; phone ahead
Telephone	(250) 391-2511
Location	2005 Sooke Road, West of Victoria, Sooke
Nearby attractions	The Royal Roads Arboretum (part of the grounds), Fort Rodd Hill National Park

wedding photographs.

The Upper Lake and Japanese Gardens were planted by a Japanese gardener. There are large pavilions, a massive pool, several winding pathways and Tortoise Island, which represents longevity. The metal cranes in the centre of the lake represent 1,000 years.

From the lakes, the property sweeps down to the ocean; Dunsmuir kept his yacht in Esquimalt Harbour. It is interesting to ponder why James, having devoted his life's energy to acquisition, became increasingly reclusive and shunned social events. Perhaps it is because his favorite son and heir, James Jr., died before him in 1915. Dunsmuir died at the age of 69 in 1920.

The Castle grounds also include an arboretum of landscape trees and border on a tidal lagoon with a wildlife sanctuary. There are scattered alpine and rock gardens, a croquet lawn with perennial borders, a native plant woodland garden and many smaller plantings. The lawns slope down to viewpoints overlooking the Straits of Juan de Fuca and the Olympic Peninsula.

Neptune: Divine Monarch of the Ocean

One statue in particular dominates Hatley Castle. Neptune stands magestically at the top of a wide staircase. According to legend, Neptune rode Hippocampus, a creature with a horse's forelegs and the tail of a fish. During his vengeful skirmishes, he split the ship of Ajax with his trident; broke Odysseus' raft; turned Phoenician ships to stone; dried up vital springs;

Known as Neptune to the Romans or Poseidon to the Greeks, this statue dominates Hatley Castle.

created the desert in Ethiopia; and started undersea earthquakes. Horses and bulls were sacrificed to appease his stormy outbursts.

In his most famous escapade, Neptune commanded the waves to produce a beautiful bull as a gift for King Minos of Crete. Perhaps Neptune's exploits struck a cord with James Dunsmuir.

Hatley Castle and Its Ghosts

There could scarcely be a castle without a ghost or two, and Hatley is no exception. Inside its stone walls, during its time as a military training academy, several cadets filed reports stating that they were shaken awake by an angry female spirit. After James' death in 1920, his wife, née Laura Surles of Georgia, lived a sheltered life at Hatley Park with her daughter Eleanor. Laura passed on in August, 1937 and, unable to keep up the estate, Eleanor died six months later—a sombre ending to a family fortune.

A masculine ghostly visitor is encountered occasionally in the gardens of Middle Lake. It is likely to be James' younger brother,

Middle Lake

Alexander (Alex) Dunsmuir, who fled to live in California. Shortly after his honeymoon, Alex's lifelong drinking excesses caught up with him, and he passed away. His young wife, Josephine, chronically ill with cancer, died two years later in 1901. She came to Victoria to mourn her husband's death. She claimed that Alex's ghost appeared periodically. It has been said that the ghostly mist that sometimes covers Hatley's Middle Lake may well be troubled Alex, searching for his bride.

Alex Dunsmuir's Oakland (CA) estate was purchased in 1906 by I.W. Hellman Jr. of the Wells Fargo Bank. In 1959, that 37-room mansion and its 19 ha (48 acre) gardens were purchased by the City of Oakland. Today, they operate as show gardens: **Dunsmuir House and Gardens**, 2960 Peralta Oaks Court, Oakland, CA, (415) 562-0328. Additionally, the town of Dunsmuir, California is named after James' brother.

Herb Gardens in British Columbia

Herb Gardens are grown for culinary purposes; Physic (also spelled Physick) Gardens are grown for therapeutic purposes. During the Middle Ages, it was the duty of rural monasteries to care for wounded travelers. Although village women grew herbs, monks had access old manuscripts called "herbals." In 1484, Guttenburg's successor, Peter Schöffer took these manuscripts and printed a Latin "Herbarius." In 1551, Jerome Bock published *Kreüterbuch*, the first book to record an author's observations. Many variations followed. In 1652, Nicolas Culpepper published *English Physitian.*

Without the benefit of scientific experimentation, early Herbals contain wildly inaccurate claims. For example, it was thought that plants resembled the parts of the body they help to cure. Nuts alleviated mental illness, claimed herbals, because they resembled the human brain.

Late in the 17th century, the science of botany developed. When subjected to scientific investigation, herbal healing proved disappointing. Hopeful scientific naval expeditions continued to collect plant samples around the world. Soon botanists were overwhelmed with the complex task of classifying their findings.

In 1673, the Worshipful Society of Apothecaries founded Chelsea Physic Garden. To the present day, it continues to grow pure herbal materials—a small 1.6 ha (3.5 acre) oasis in the heart of London that supplies herbs for researchers around the world. Vancouver's

A stone bench at the Raven Hill Herb Farm is ruffled with woolly thyme.

U.B.C. Physick Garden is stocked largely from Chelsea Physic Garden. In Vancouver, a small herb garden intended for research into Asian-Buddhist Alternative Medicine is the Tzu Chi Institute, located at 767 West 12th Avenue. The largest medicinal herb garden in the western hemisphere, first established in 1911, is located near British Columbia in Seattle, Washington. Phone: (206) 543-1126.

Approximately 25 per cent of all modern prescription drugs contain active ingredients that were initially identified in plants. The US National Cancer Institute recently dis-

Medieval herbalists knew of aloe, a succulent cactus used to soothe burns.

covered mild antitumor properties in about 7,000 plants. Taxol, derived from Pacific yew tree bark and Vincristine from Madagascar periwinkle are both promising anti-cancer agents.

Herb and Physick Gardens in British Columbia

Helmcken House Garden	Physick	Victoria
Park & Tilford Gardens	Herb	North Vancouver
Raven Hill Herb Farm	Herb	Saanichton
Sooke Harbour House	Herb	Sooke
Tzu Chi Institute	Physick	Vancouver
U.B.C. Botanical Gardens	Physick	Vancouver
VanDusen Botanical Garden	Herb	Vancouver

Herb Gardens: Greater Victoria

Raven Hill in early spring

Sooke Harbour House

Raven Hill Herb Farm

At Raven Hill Farm, herbs grow together in a variety of garden tapestries. Bouquets of fennel and pungent dill vie for attention with creeping thyme and savory. Noel Richardson and her husband, Andrew Yeoman, have farmed this location for almost 20 years. They learned to mix flowers, herbs and vegetables into myriads of colours, textures and designs. The first bit of conventional wisdom they threw away is that all herbs thrive in desert-like conditions. On the contrary, they discovered that most herbs love the moist climate near Victoria. While cookbook author Noel experiments with herbs in the kitchen, Andrew tends a menagerie of pheasants, goats, chickens, sheep, peacocks and a noisy donkey. They both tend the garden, giving it generous helpings of organic compost. Andrew has a penchant for stone benches, brick walls, half barrels and all the accoutrements that make an herb garden wonderful. The owners sell bedding herbs as well as full-grown herbal enticements. The terraced garden overlooking Brentwood Bay is the source of many of the herbs used in regional restaurants, and is open to the public on Sunday afternoons. Phone for information; (250) 652-4024.

Location: 330 Mt. Newton Crossroad, R.R. #2, Saanichton.

Sooke Harbour House Gardens

Sooke Harbour House, a small inn and restaurant, sits on the edge of a long spit in the Strait of Juan de Fuca. When the sky is clear, the Olympic Mountains form a majestic backdrop for the herb-and-flower gardens. Owners Philip and Frederica Sinclair have developed a specialty garden to cater to their restaurant. Here, they serve strictly local delicacies flavoured with fresh herbs and edible flowers.

If you choose to stay for dinner or overnight, one of four chefs will create a unique meal. Nasturtium flowers, for example, add an elegant touch to salads tossed with apple cider and local hazelnut oils. You may be surprised to find tulip or pansy petals rolled into your ravioli pasta. Several varieties of dried seaweeds are served, and you might find pear and ox-eye daisy sorbet on the menu. The oceanfront garden itself is open for unobtrusive public browsing during daylight hours. Reservations for the restaurant or overnight are compulsory; (250) 642-3421. Admission is free to the private gardens. Wheelchair: mostly accessible.

Location: 1528 Whiffen Spit Road, Sooke.

Horticultural Centre of the Pacific: Saanich

In 1975, the municipality of Saanich, near Victoria, set aside 43 ha (106 acres) of wetland to promote plant research and education. Today, this reserve includes a natural area, a demonstration garden and a new arboretum. Horticultural students and their teachers make good use of the training and demonstration garden located onsite. Apparently designed by a series of committees, these gardens have a patchwork-type of charm.

Certification as a Horticultural Technician in Garden Maintenance and Design takes one year to complete. The program includes guest lectures, small business practices, basic gardening instruction, plant recognition and culture, 500 hours of practical experience, and field trips to local horticultural establishments and private gardens. Part-time instructors at the Centre teach to up to 18 students. Their expertise is supplemented by appropriate specialists from the community. The outdoor instruction section is carried out by two full-time professional gardeners and a part-time instructor.

Many visitors drop by the Horticulture Centre of the Pacific to inspect mature examples of plants they are considering for their own gardens. The information booth is rarely staffed, so most visitors wander around by themselves. Some of the sub-gardens include the Winter Garden, Heather Garden, a newly established Japanese Garden

This training garden is popular for its public plant sales.

and a partially labeled perennial collection. Lilies, Michaelmas daisies, rhododendrons and irises are abundant in season.

Information: Horticultural Centre	
Type	A registered trade school teaching garden operated by a registered non-profit organization and open to the public.
Size	43 ha (106 acre) reserve of which 8 ha (20 acres) are cultivated gardens
Time allotment	45 minutes to 1 hour
Open	8 a.m. to dusk
Year-round	Yes
Best seasons	Late spring, summer, autumn
Sub-gardens	Winter Garden, Rose arbor, Rhododendron groves, perennial flowerbeds, Japanese garden, Heather Garden
Additional facilities	Public washrooms; no dining
Events	Workshops, lectures, plant sales; the Centre offers workshops and monthly "Garden Talks" on various horticultural topics. There are special Plant Sale Days
Admission charged	Yes, $2 or more by donation
Wheelchair access	Mostly accessible
Guided tours	Not normally; special horticultural lectures can be arranged
Telephone	(250) 479-6162
Location	505 Quayle Road, Saanich
Nearby attractions	Bird reserve and new arboretum

Victoria's Knot Garden

Knot Garden: Victoria

A parterre garden is characterized by well-ordered geometric patterns. Largely two-dimensional, parterres are designed to emphasize the ground plane. Consisting of a mathematical "bonework," they can take several forms: the English Knot garden, Maze or Labyrinth Gardens, formal French Garden or Carpet Bedding. All draw heavily on the basic technique of translating a geometric pattern into an elegant, high-maintenance garden using distinctly coloured plants, clipped hedges, coloured glass, coloured earth, sand, gravel, or flowers. Usually, a hillside or overhead vantage point, called a "mount," is required to appreciate their intricacy.

A Knot Garden is a good example of parterre. Common in aristocratic English gardens during the 16th and 17th centuries, but most often associated with the earlier Elizabethan period, they consist of interlacing bands of vegetation formed by a low-growing hedges. Box hedge, rosemary or thyme are used for the framework, and the spaces are filled with flowers or herbs. Certain knot designs are standard. For example, The Tradescant knot, a central square enclosed within a circle, is named after John Tradescant (d. 1638), an English traveller and the earliest known garden-plant collector. Other designs emulate a brocade weaver's elaborate designs.

A small Knot Garden (spelled Knott in England) and its mount are found in central Victoria near the Centennial Fountain. This is a fitting garden to be included in the cacophony of British-style gardens here. Also located in the vicinity of Centennial Square is a statue of Sir John A. MacDonald, Canada's first Prime Minister. He once came to Victoria via the newly built Canadian Pacific Railway, and attended a garden party at Point Ellice gardens; see page 47. Admission is free. The area is wheelchair accessible.

Location: 1 Centennial Square, 1600 block off Douglas Street, Victoria.

Garden Events in Victoria Information

With more than 20 garden societies, three official garden clubs, hundreds of unofficial clubs, and the Friends of the University Garden Association, there are thousands of avid gardeners to attend Victoria's annual shows, garden parties and plant sales. For information on upcoming events, please consult the following:

Times-Colonist newspaper weekly listings	Consult the newspaper
Tourism Victoria	(250) 361-9733
Victoria Conservatory of Music, garden tours	(250) 386-5311, (250) 592-0855
Victoria Flower & Garden Festival, mid-June	(250) 920-5925
Victoria Horticultural Society	**(250) 592-8618**
Victoria Visitor InfoCentre	(250) 953-2033

Native Plant Gardens: Victoria

The grounds surrounding the Royal British Columbia Museum provide a setting for guided interpretive plant-identification programs and drop-in visits. In 1968, museum botanists began to collect plants to illustrate four vegetation zones:

1) Coast Forest Zone: dense coniferous forest
2) Dry Interior Zone: south-central, semi-desert shrub-lands
3) Alpine Zone: high mountain elevations
4) Wetland Zone: peat bogs and marshes

Like the artifacts inside the museum, this plant collection adds a dynamic dimension to the museum's indoor Natural History Galleries. To get the most out of the outer garden, pick up a "Native Plant

Coastal Forest Zone Identification

Gardens" brochure at the museum entrance and follow the diagrams. They identify key plants in each vegetation zone. Find the flowering Pacific dogwood, delicate blue camas lilies—a favourite food for aboriginals and early settlers, and the 3-petal trillium, an outstanding wildflower. Admission to the grounds is free. Allow 30 minutes for a comprehensive visit. The area is wheelchair accessible.

Location: Beside and around the Royal British Columbia Museum, 675 Belleville Street.

Is There a Distinctive Pacific Coast Garden Style?

To illustrate the northwest Pacific coast garden style, a recent television series entitled "Northwest Gardens" explored several private and semi-public gardens in the region. All public British Columbia gardens mentioned in this series are covered in this book. The following are examined in the television series.

• S. Pearl/B. Sacks Garden, Bainbridge Island, WA, a child-friendly garden
• Willoughby Garden, Portland, OR, a bird-friendly cottage garden
• Arthur Erickson Garden, Vancouver, a Japanese-style water garden
• Francisca Darts Garden, Surrey, a vast plant collection

• Phoebe Noble Garden, Victoria, a private, overgrown English garden
• two Bill Overholt Gardens, WA,
a) busy urban setting,
b) perennial borders at a country retreat
• J. Kroft Garden, Cannon Beach, OR, an artist's seaside cottage
• The Olmsted Legacy
a) Stamper Garden, Seattle, Estate Garden,
b) Bishop's Close, Portland, a grand European estate
• Platt Garden, Portland, OR, a Weaver's Texture Garden
• Feeney Garden, Bellingham, WA, a 1901 lakeside cottage
• Georges Garden, Portland, perennials and hardscapes
• Community Gardens, Victoria

and Seattle, features communal urban gardening
• P. Stockwell, Seattle, a Lake Union Houseboat Garden
• Wiltermood Garden, Port Orchard, a wetland garden
• Sooke Harbour House, Sooke, an oceanside herb & culinary garden
• Campbell Garden, Bainbridge Island, WA, a creative water-wise garden
• J. Kenyon Garden, Redmond, WA, a blurred Japanese design
• T. Hobbs (private) Garden, Vancouver, a sizzling Mediterranean-villa garden
• The Miller Garden, Seattle, a thousand harmonious plants.

Parks with Gardens: Victoria

Beacon Hill Park

This well-loved grand-daddy of all Victoria's Parks was designed by Scots-born landscape architect John Blare. After winning an 1889 competition, he planted several hybrid rhododendrons around Fountain Lake. More than 100 years later, they remain spectacular. Blare designed several cultivated beds including a Fragrance Garden and a fine array of spring bulbs and annuals. Additionally, visitors can enjoy a petting zoo, formal Rose Garden, or an outdoor summer concert at the band shell. Victoria's Alpine Society cultivates an Alpine Garden. Visitors often bring a few crumbs for the ducks, who preen themselves on one of the three mini-lakes. Admission is free, and the area is wheelchair accessible.

Location: Douglas Street leads into Beacon Hill Park.

Playfair Park

In late April, this park's rhododendrons are in full bloom, and in May a hillside of blue camas lilies bursts into bloom.

Admission is free, and the area is wheelchair: accessible.

Location: Cumberland Street and Judge Avenue.

Saxe Point Park

Famous for its spring bulbs, perennial beds and flowering shrubs, this park is located near the ocean. The coastal forest features expanses of grass in a syl-

Clockwise from top left: Beacon Hill Park; Playfair Park, blue camas fields; Saxe Point Park; University of Victoria Gardens

van setting. A tiny handkerchief tree will someday be the park's centrepiece, but in the mean time, neatly cultivated beds adorn the area. Cars arrive intermittently, picnickers stop awhile, and many stroll the area, taking in the salt air. Admission is free, and the area is wheelchair accessible.

Location: At the foot of Fraser Street.

University of Victoria Grounds

Home to the imported English Meadowlark, this little feathered creature's dulcet tones can often be heard as visitors wander around the display gardens that decorate this university campus. Rhododendrons and azaleas are the primary species featured at UVic's Finnerty Garden. Nearby are a number "native plant" gardens, containing imported perennials that university gardeners could not resist adding. Garden bed displays change from year to year, and make for enjoyable summer meandering. Admission is free, and the area is wheelchair accessible.

Location: In and around Interfaith Chapel, University of Victoria Campus, north of Cedar Hill Cross Road and west of Henderson Road.

British Columbia Rhododendrons

Representatives of this genus are found on all continents of the world except South America and tropical Africa. From the mid-1800s to the late 1920s, both Britain and America funded botany expeditions to the Himalayas, China and Japan. Many of today's common domestic rhododendrons are hybrids of the wild stock collected during that period. One variety of wild rhododendron grows in British Columbia and is protected by law. Called the "Pacific rhododendron," the Rh. macrophyllum escaped extinction during the last ice age, about 30,000 years ago. Scattered patches thrive deep in the forest at Manning Park near Hope, and near Rhododendron Lake on Vancouver Island. Both locations are described in this book. Five hybrids of B.C.'s wild plant are found in public gardens, the most notable of which is Rh. Albert Close.

Rhododendrons thrive best in the acidic soil of coniferous forests. B.C.'s coastal growers have been exceptionally successful with

Finnerty Garden, Victoria

B.C.'s own wild Rhododendron, Rh. macrophyllum

Domestic Hybrid, "Cosmopolitan Pink"

this bell-shaped flower. Because it is relatively easy to hybridize, a

number of talented gardeners have also created new cultivars.

Finnerty Garden: Victoria

With the goal of becoming the definitive rhododendron and azalea display garden in Victoria, Finnerty Garden was planted in 1974 with a bequest from the estate of Jeanne Buchanan Simpson of Cowichan Lake. She and her husband George were notable collectors of rhododendrons. The Simpson Collection was, at one time, the largest in British Columbia. Many of its original plants were grown from seeds obtained in the 1920s

from Asiatic plant explorers. After a time, the collection was transferred to a boggy, 1.2 ha (3 acre) site on the university campus. Subsequently, the non-profit Victoria Finnerty Garden Friends have had their challenges planning, developing, nursing and relocating the specimens in this garden.

Today, a number of 75-year-old distorted rhodo-giants, mostly *Rh. fortunei* from the mountains of Asia struggle along, well

past their prime, but still of significant historical value. A new garden section dedicated to B.C. hybrids is being assembled, and fresh contributions add to its splendour in late April and May. Garden tours are held from time to time. Admission is free. The area is wheelchair accessible.

Location: Interfaith Chapel, University of Victoria, north of Cedar Hill Cross Road and west of Henderson Road.

British Columbia Rhododendrons

VanDusen Gardens' Rhododendron Walk: Vancouver

Century Gardens, Burnaby's rhododendron garden

Collector's Rhododendron, Rh. Simpson

blotches and markings. Today, azaleas are also considered to be a form of rhododendron.

Information about British Columbia's rhododendron breeders, their hybridized cultivars, and the location of private rhododendron gardens is being compiled. Harry Wright of Haida Gold Gardens in Courtenay is currently taking inventory. So far, he has catalogued about 100 dedicated B.C. gardeners and over 3,300 varieties. He is pleased to share his findings: call (250) 338-8345. A few B.C. garden associations and university enthusiasts are also working to further rhododendron-related research, and to make the information accessible to the public.

In the meantime, there are several wonderful public gardens dedicated to rhododendrons and those who appreciate the lush, flowing shrub have ample opportunity to enjoy superb displays in season (from mid-April to early May). Local newspapers also report on private garden owners who offer to "leave the gate open" and allow visitors to walk through their fields of bell flowers.

Some have been credited for their efforts by the American Rhododendron Society; see page 73.

Classifying the world's 800 species of rhododendrons and their hybrids has been referred to "a taxonomist's nightmare." They come in a range of sizes and colours and display myriads of

Rhododendron Display Gardens in B.C.

The following public gardens feature large displays of rhododendrons best viewed from mid-April to mid-May. Private gardeners often open their gates to visitors as well.

Bear Creek Garden	Surrey	Hailey Rhododendron Grove	Nanaimo
Butchart Gardens	Victoria	Minter Gardens	Rosedale
Century Gardens	Burnaby	Queen Elizabeth Park	Vancouver
Fantasy Garden World	Richmond	Park and Tilford Gardens	North Vancouver
Finnerty Gardens	UVic Campus, Victoria	Playfair Park	Victoria
Greig Rhododendron Garden	Stanley Park	Tofino Gardens (private)	Tofino
		U.B.C. Botanical Garden	Vancouver
		Beacon Hill Park	Victoria
		VanDusen Botanical Gardens	Vancouver
		Filburg Lodge	Comox

The Language of Flowers

In 1842, Lady Mary Wortley Montagu started a craze in England during which flower language threatened to replace the written word among young lovers. During a stay in Istanbul, she sent a widely publicized "Turkish love letter." Her so-called "word posy" included shocking hidden messages: a clove, "I have long loved you secretly;" a jonquil, "Have pity on my passion;" a strawflower, "I am your slave;" a peppercorn, "Send me an answer."

According to Montagu, it was possible to send a message "without inking the fingers." For two decades, this custom was wildly popular and was largely responsible for the birth of the florist industry. Based on Shakespearean literature and fanciful folklore, more than 50 newly published books allowed friends and lovers to interpret each other's secret flower messages. Young ladies thumbing through the *Language of Flowers* eagerly deciphered their latest bouquets.

The art could be tricky. Not only flowers, but the tilt of knots in binding ribbons conveyed meaning. Ribbons tilted to the right directed the message at the receiver while those that tilted left addressed the giver.

Years after the decline of "tussie mussies," particular sentiments are still associated with different kinds of flowers. A red rose signifies ardent love, a daisy signifies innocence.

About 150 years ago, lovers exchanged bouquets carefully chosen to convey encoded messages. Deep pink roses were sent to express gratitude and appreciation.

Victorian-era Language of Flowers

A Mushroom	Suspicion is all around us.
Buttercups	What childishness!
Chrysanthemum	You have slighted me. I am offended.
Daisy	Celebrate your innocence and freedom.
Deep pink rose	Accept my gratitude and appreciation.
Deep red carnation	Alas, my poor heart breaks.
Gardenias	You are lovely and charming.
Holly	Am I forgotten?
Hydrangea	You heartless boaster.
Iris	Look for a written message from me.
Ivy	Marriage? My faithful fidelity is yours.
Light pink rose	I have sympathy for your plight.
Mixed pale roses	Accept my friendship and meet me.
Orange, peach rose	My deep enthusiasm borders on desire.
Orchid	You are very beautiful.
Peonies	For shame, for shame, for shame.
Purple lilac	I feel the first stirrings of love within me.
Red & yellow roses	I am overflowing with love for you.
Red rose	I ardently love and respect you.
	My true love, you are the one.
Red tulip	I wish to make a declaration now: I love you.
Rhubarb leaves	Quick! I need your advice.
Tulips, assorted	You are so vain.
Violets	I am ever faithful.
White & red roses	Let us be united forever, dearest.
White rose	You fill me with reverence and humility.
	Let us love in secret.
White rose buds	You are too young to know of love.
Yellow carnation	I disdain you.
Yellow rose	Between lovers: Do not be suspicious of me.
	Between women: Be careful, the one you love may be unfaithful.

Flowering trees abounded in the O'Reilly family's garden more than 100 years ago.

The O'Reilly Family and friends, 1870; the gentlemen include an Admiral (back) with Mr. and Mrs. O'Reilly (seated), two Royal Navy Captains (Kathleen's suitors?) and son Frank O'Reilly; daughter Kathleen is in the centre.

Point Ellice House Heirloom Gardens: Victoria

"This really is a living history museum," explains former head gardener, Carolyn Herriot. "The period house is over 125 years old, and its gardens represent their heyday from 1889 to 1914." Although several decades of neglect and the pollution of heavy industry once threatened to destroy this 0.9 ha (2.2 acre) site, this lot on Pleasant Street has made a comeback. Once again it reflects upper middle-class living. The gardens of Point Ellice House provide a special opportunity to experience gardens restored to Victorian and Edwardian-era specifications. Under the direction of knowledgeable heritage gardeners, the authentic period gardens are as healthy as they were more than a century ago.

Built in 1862, the Italianate house was passed down through several generations of the O'Reilly family. Peter O'Reilly, a native of County Meath, Ireland, was appointed as Gold Commissioner for the all-important Cariboo District during the 1860s gold rush. The O'Reillys raised two boys and a girl in an atmosphere dominated by riding events, tennis matches, family outings, garden parties, open houses, afternoon teas and picnics. By 1976, 100 years later, the estate's heirs could no longer afford the upkeep, and the provincial government took it on as a heritage property. Luckily, the O'Reillys never threw anything out. Thousands of items were packed away in their cavernous barn, basement and attics. Today's restorative gardeners are able to resurrect terra cotta forcing pots, old racks, cold frames, glass cloches, latticework trellises, bricks and garden tools. They are able to read detailed logs of every garden activity, and even try to germinate "saved" seeds.

Like many late Victorians, the O'Reilly family considered the genteel pastime of gardening to be physically, morally and spiritually uplifting. Peter Sr. laid out the basic hardscape, planting holly, ivy and laurel, and ordered trees including maple, redwood, mountain ash and horse chestnut. His eldest daughter, Charlotte Kathleen (Kit), devoted her life to detailing the grounds. She kept journals about planting lilacs, jasmine, moss roses and English hawthorne. In addition to caring for dozens of annuals including sweetpeas

47

and cornflowers, she and a few servants tended 60 varieties of roses in a heart-shaped garden. She cultivated an archway of honeysuckle near the carriage entrance. The kitchen garden also occupied much of their time.

Since Point Ellice became a protected heritage property in 1976, its restoration has been remarkable. The overgrown, neglected garden was a jumbled mess, but living treasures lay in wait. First, the curving gravel paths, ornate trellises and formal brick separators were uncovered. The small barn was rebuilt to original specifications. Clippings of original ivy, holly, false cypress and laurel were propagated. Overgrowth obscuring the scenic vista toward Selkirk Water was cleared and the croquet and tennis lawns were elevated to period standards. Old plants and roses mentioned in O'Reilly journals were ordered from specialty houses in Great Britain. In 1977, complete inventories of the property's annuals, biennials, perennials, bulbs, shrubs and climbing plants were compiled. In the newly pruned environment, several period plants suddenly sprang back to life. The most remarkable of these were the pre-1920, four m (12 foot) hollyhocks. Dormant for decades in The Woodland Walk, these heirloom plants now bloom late each summer. Heritage seeds from these hollyhocks are available for sale on site.

Point Ellice House and Gardens are owned and maintained by the Province of British Columbia and presented to the public by the Victoria Rediscovery Society. The gardens consist of The Woodland Walk, Croquet Lawn, Flower Gardens, South Garden, Carriage Drive, Barn and Ferry Dock. The partially restored house is open for guided tours; tours of the Victorian-era garden are self-guided. Point Ellice sponsors art classes, garden workshops, photography classes and an annual Heritage Plant Sale; phone for details (250) 380-6506. Admission is charged. The garden is wheelchair accessible; the house is not. Afternoon tea is served in the garden.

Location: 2616 Pleasant Street, Victoria.

Kathleen O'Reilly, A Darling Gardener

No belle ever had more dashing suitors than darling Charlotte Kathleen (Kit) O'Reilly, yet she ended her days a spinster in the house where she was born (1867-1945). To this day, Kit's life leaves many unanswered questions, particularly about her relationship with young Lieutenant Robert Scott, a determined man who made his mark in history. During his Royal Navy posting to Esquimalt in the 1890s, both Kathleen's letters and her father's diaries record Scott's frequent visits to Point Ellice. We assume that he (as well as at least one other suitor) proposed to her one evening along The Woodland Walk, likely in the vicinity of the hollyhocks. What happened is a mystery, but Scott married someone else. Kathleen built a heart-shaped garden filled with roses, one of which

Kathleen (Kit) O'Reilly once rejected the amorous advances of soon-to-be famous South Pole explorer, Captain Robert Scott.

was an old white rose called "the bride." Since obscure Old Roses are stylish again, "The bride" was recently discovered in a specialty nursery in Great Britain and replanted in the revived South Garden.

Kit rejected another suitor: old Commander Henry Athole Scudamore Stanhope, future Earl of Chesterfield. In his case, she wrote to her father saying his advances frightened her and that she didn't want her life to change: "I love being here with you all, and though you may think I am discontented, ... I do not believe .. anyone has ever had a happier home life than I have..." As to Robert Scott, he perished in the coldest place on earth in 1912, commanding an expedition to reach Antarctica's South Pole.

How Does Your Victorian Food Garden Grow?

Sea Kale, a Victorian-era vegetable no longer popular, grows in Point Ellice's historically accurate kitchen garden. It was considered a delicacy to be served only when guests came to dinner. Its flavour is described as a delicate "nutty asparagus."

From records kept by the O'Reillys, this is what they grew. Today, some varieties can be obtained from specialty seed sources; others are lost.

Autumn king cabbage or walking stick cabbage

Country gentlemen corn

English vegetable marrow

Fertilizers of compost, lime, leaf mulch, fall rye, okra-tofu

Flowers for indoor house bouquets mint,

Green curled Scotch dark kale

Harlington Windsor broad bean bush

Horsford Market Garden peas

Medicinal herb beds

Picwik gooseberries

Scarlet runner beans

Veitch's autumn giant cauliflower

White globe purple top turnip

Earliest short horn carrots

Empress of India cucumber

Citron small green melon

Rhubarb

Savory herb bed: lavender, sage, thyme

Grand Rapids lettuce

Early round pod Valentine bean

New Enormous tomato

Royal sovereign strawberries

Black currants and raspberries

Deep red blood beet

Paris golden yellow celery

Prickly spinach

Ghosts in the Garden

Dozens of ghostly encounters have occurred at Point Ellice. Two Australian nurses, surreptitiously camping in The Woodland, fled when a specter screamed "Get out!". One ghost followed two male visitors down a lane; another acted as a silent "tour guide;" another frightened a child so badly her mother threatened to sue. The cleaning staff periodically hears clearly articulated but outdated orders through a closed door, when no one is in the room.

In 1971, American psychic Ms. H. Smith was called in to investigate. She found the garden and house to contain several presences including traces of Kathleen and her mother. As recently as 1994, during the Commonwealth Games in Victoria,

The Woodland Walk at Point Ellice, depicted here in 1902, is partially intact today and has been the site of several ghostly encounters. It is likely the famous Robert Scott proposed to Kathleen O'Reilly in this vicinity. The child shown here is merely called Gwen.

the Canadian Broadcasting Corporation (CBC) was filming here. According to some observers, a swirling vortex and a globe—a small, ball-shaped light—appeared on their news footage. Point Ellice's former head gardener, Carolyn Herriot, is matter-of-fact. She affirms that it must be Kit who shimmers through The Woodland Walk on summer afternoons and evenings. Perhaps she is repeating her youth, inspecting her garden, or reliving the details of her rejected suitors' marriage proposals. Point Ellice holds a special public event each Halloween to retell its ghostly tales. There are several books documenting Point Ellice's ghostly visitors.

Tea in the Garden: Point Ellice

As in the "gay nineties," afternoon tea is a strict custom throughout the summer. Those who come for tea follow in the footsteps of many a distinguished guest. In 1886, Sir John A. MacDonald crossed the country by rail and came to Point Ellice for tea. He stayed for an evening garden party, reported to be an idyllic summer evening, with glowing lanterns and fireflies lighting up the flowers. Of course, Lieutenant Robert Scott also accepted many a teacup from the servants and no doubt made eyes at young Kathleen, exactly where you sit in the sun taking your "cuppa." If you are a history aficionado, ask the tea server to see the archival photographs of the O'Reilly family. For your pleasure, wooden croquet mallets and balls are on the lawn, and as long as you know how to play, you are welcome to swing away. Attendants are dressed in period costume; the head gardener will answer your questions.

Two staff members hearken back to the Edwardian-era. Server Emily Holmes presents Mistress Marlis Schweitzer with her afternoon repast. Below: Afternoon Tea in the Garden at Point Ellice.

Visitors may also take the tiny Harbour Ferry, travelling from the float in front of the Empress Hotel to Point Ellice and back again.

Reservations are recommended; phone Point Ellice House, (250) 380-6506. Afternoon tea and light lunch are served outdoors, weather permitting, in summer, 11 a.m. to 4 p.m. The garden is

wheelchair accessible; the house is not.

Location: 2616 Pleasant Street, Victoria.

The Three "Hs" of Old Gardens: Point Ellice

A hollyhock cultivar suddenly sprang back to life in 1984.

Heirloom	Most valuable of all, these are actual old-era plants, bushes or that have survived for a century or more. In effect, we inherit them.	The original Lilac bush by the back door at Point Ellice
Heritage	Offspring from an era's original plants: shoots, seeds, cuttings.	Hollyhock Heritage Seeds taken from original plants on site
Historic	True to a certain time period; a plant exactly like the species that would have grown during an era. Researchers source these from genetic seedbanks.	Old varieties of roses and vegetables no longer in fashion

Keefer Farms
&
Greenhouses

Richmond, B.C.
Retail Sales

DIRECT FROM GROWER

HUNDREDS TO CHOOSE FROM

BEAUTIFUL FLOWERING
HANGING BASKET &
CONTAINER SPECIALISTS
FOR OVER 20 YEARS

...take a little beauty home with you.

Flowerful Arrays

To take a little beauty home with you, stroll through our greenhouses and enjoy the wonderful selection of flowers. Whether you are looking for a familiar favourite, searching for something new, or need help finding the right basket for the sun or shade of your home and garden, take a moment to talk to us.

We'll help you choose the variety and colours that are right for you. Amongst the flowerful arrays of popular plants and exciting new species you'll find at Keefer Farms & Greenhouses are:

Bacopa	Bidens
Brachycome	Convolvulus
Diascia	Helichrysum
Calcoelaria	Schizanthus
Heliotrope	Ice Plant
Lobelia Ricardii	Lotus Vine
Streptacarpella	Cerinthe Major
Million Bells	Scaevola
Silver Nettle	Supertunias
Torenia	Wadelia
Verbian(Tapien and Temari)	

We also use many varieties of geraniums and fuschias.

"From Victorian side planted moss baskets to a large selection of contemporary baskets, containers and planter boxes, Dan and Donna search for new ways to mingle old favorites you love with new and exciting varieties you'll be pleased to discover."

Basket Varieties

12" Side Planted Moss Hanging Baskets
14" Side Planted Moss Hanging Baskets
16" Side Planted Moss Hanging Baskets
18" Side Planted Moss Hanging Baskets
14" Side Planted Moss Wall Basket

14" Side Planted Octagonal Cedar Hanging Basket
15" Rectangular Cedar Hanging Basket
12" Square Cedar Hanging Basket

24" Cedar Window Box
36" Cedar Window Box
48" Cedar Window Box

12" Plastic (Mixed) Hanging Basket
10" Plastic (Mixed) Hanging Basket
10" Plastic (All Ivy Geraniums or All Fuschia)
     Hanging Basket
8" Plastic (Mixed) Hanging Basket

... and a bountiful selection of colour bowls and tubs,
clay pots and cedar planter boxes.

Open every Spring from the last Weekend in April
through June (while supply lasts)

Keefer Farms & Greenhouses
17080 Cambie Road
Richmond, BC V6V 1H1
ph. 278-8943 fax. 270-8694

Leave the city behind you and enter anther world. Located in North-East Richmond, the idyllic setting of Keefer Farms and Greenhouses is just a short drive away. Nestled amongst tall shady trees and distant mountains, surrounded by fresh green fields and lawns, a beautiful oasis of flowers awaits you.

Take your time to wander through our many greenhouses. An exotic assortment of colours and frangances will delight your senses. Keefer Farms and Greenhouses have been in the family for three generations. For the past twenty years, Dan and Donna Keefer have been growing and desiginig their unique variety of hanging baskets. From Victorian side planted moss baskets to a large selection of contemporaty baskets, patio containers and planter boxes, Dan and Donna search for new ways to mingle the old favourites you love with new and exciting varities you'll be pleased to discover.

Rose Gardens: Victoria

Ada G. Beaven Memorial Rose Garden

"A rose is a rose is a rose," wrote American author Gertrude Stein, but is this so? There are hundreds of varieties of roses with a tremendous array of growth habits, shapes and sizes, as well as many different leaf and flower colours, forms and textures. Named after dedicated rosarian Ada B. Beaven (1867-1958), this small rose garden features an assortment of hybrid teas and floribundas. Ada was a contemporary of Kathleen (Kit) O'Reilly of Point Ellice. Admission is free, and the area is wheelchair accessible.

Location: Newport Avenue and Currie Road.

Ada G. Beaven Memorial Rose Garden

Empress Hotel Rose Garden

"The rose bloom unfolds elegantly, having a pointed center, with petals spiraling out in layers. A slowly opening bud is at its "artistic best" when it is one-half to three-quarters open, with its tight center still closed, petals furling out, dewy fresh and full of life." So goes one description of the rose, a flower that has completely captivated our affection. After a summer's afternoon tea in the Empress Hotel Lobby, enjoy a stroll in the rose garden, always open. Admission is free and the area is wheelchair accessible.

Location: On the grounds of the Empress Hotel, 721 Government Street.

The Empress Hotel

Government House

Oak Bay

Government House Rose Gardens

Maintained by environmentally friendly means, the sweeping gardens of the Lieutenant-Governor's mansion culminate in formal Rose Gardens, a favourite with many past Lieutenant-Governors' wives. Always a popular stop for bridal parties, the sunny gardens are in full bloom in June and early July. Colonists brought the first roses to North America in the 16th century, and they were introduced to Victoria shortly after European colonization began in the 1840s. This makes the rose one of the oldest cultivated European plants in the region. Modern rose hybrids date back to the 1860s, when an extensive hybridizing program was carried out. By 1920, hybrid teas dominated the market. They remain the most popular rose variety today. Admission is free and the area is wheelchair accessible.

Location: 1401 Rockland Avenue.

Oak Bay Rose Gardens

Shakespeare referred to flowers' mysterious meanings in several of his plays. The classic red rose is said to mean "I ardently love and respect you. My true love, you are the one." Also on display here is the most popular cultivar ever, the "peace rose." Admission is free and the area is wheelchair accessible.

Location: Estevan and Thompson Avenue.

Wild rose, northern hemisphere

Rosemania, ancient Rome, 100 BC

An old-style rose

- 30 million years ago wild roses grew throughout the northern hemisphere.
- By 5000 BC, Mesopotamians mention roses on their clay tablets.
- By 2700 BC, Chinese Emperor Chinnun has a rose garden.
- By 1800 BC, designers paint roses inside Crete's Palace of Knossos.
- By 1500 BC, wreaths of Damask roses are placed in Egyptian tombs.
- By 1200 BC, the Greek philosopher Epicurus keeps a rose garden; Poetess Sappho

calls it "Queen of Flowers."
- From 100 BC onward, ancient Romans use roses to carpet banquet halls, add to wine, mix into cosmetics and make into garlands. Nero gives a banquet; roses flood down from the ceiling and several guests suffocate.
- By 100 AD, Persians extract the famous "attar of roses."
- In 1272, returning Crusaders bring rose trees home. Christians use roses in processions as symbols of Christian martyr's blood and the Virgin Mary.

- During the 1300s, medieval cathedrals feature rose windows.
- As an heraldic symbol in England, the War of the Roses is waged
- In 1530, King Henry VIII builds a rose garden at Hampton Court for his "awne darling" Ann Boleyn. In the Elizabethan era, Shakespeare claims, "Of all flowres, methinks a rose is best."
- By the late 1600s, breeders from the Netherlands hybridize the ten best known European rose cultivars into

Persian roses, 1600s

Empress Josephine, Queen of Roses, 1800s

Quest for a yellow hybrid, 1830s

A Brief History of Roses

Medieval rose window,1300s

Henry VIII and his Tudor roses, 1500s

Elizabethan era, 1590s

about 100 varieties.
- By 1700, Mogul emperors in India stock their gardens with imported Chinese and Persian roses.
- By 1776, India is sending roses to collectors in America.
- In 1792, the "Four Stud Chinas"—ever-blooming roses developed in China—reach Europe.
- In 1799, Josephine, Empress of France, and wife of Napoleon, builds a rose garden at Malmaison.
- By the 1820s, botanists crossbreed Asian roses with

European varieties.
- In 1876, England's new Royal National Rose Society develops the most brightly coloured roses in history.
- In 1940, a yellow-pink bloom, is reputedly smuggled out of France on the last airplane to America before German occupation. The "peace rose" sells by the millions.
- Starting in the 1960s, Canadian agricultural research centres develop the hardy "Canadian Explorer" series.
- According to florist industry statistics, more roses are sold

on Valentine's Day than on Mother's Day.
- Rose Gardens are the most popular garden attraction in the world.

Peace rose, 1940s

Portland International Rose Test Gardens

20th century's hybrid tea

A Brief History of English Tea

• In 1657, London holds its first-ever tea auction with claims that "tea makes the body lusty."

• By 1732, an evening spent watching fireworks in Vauxhall or Ranelagh Gardens is concluded with a cup of tea. Tea gardens open throughout England. A locked wooden box inscribed "T.I.P.S."—"To Insure Prompt Service" is found on each outdoor table.

• Throughout the late 1700s in Canada's New France, coffee and chocolate are popular. As *coureurs des bois* move west, tea and sugar become the dietary staples.

• By 1800, the influential English Duchess of Bedford sips her mid-afternoon tea in a hotel lounge to stave off a "sinking feeling." For 200 years, elegant hotels from London to Singapore and from Nigeria to Victoria follow suit.

• In the 1830s, British Temperance Reformers sponsor "tea parties" to combat alcohol consumption. This lays the groundwork for tea rooms—the only public places where unchaperoned women can meet friends without compromising their reputations.

• In 1844, English plant collector Robert Fortune, a fluent speaker of Mandarin, disguises himself as a Chinese native and steals the closely guarded secrets of tea cultivation.

• Ships race to transport tea to lucrative British markets. Of American design, Tea Clippers—fast, billowing sail ships—suddenly arrive on the

Afternoon tea in the garden originated in the 1850s

scene, cutting previous sailing times in half. Britain's response is to build the *Cutty Sark*.

• By 1850, attendants serve afternoon tea in drawing rooms throughout the British Empire.

• Canada's transcontinental railroad, built between 1865 and 1890, is conceived to transport tea. The proposal is to unload Asiatic tea in Vancouver, transport it quickly across the country by rail, reload in Montreal and sail rapidly to England. Canada, a loyal British Colony, has preferential tariffs with Britain and investors count on

undercutting the Americans. Unfortunately, the Canadian Pacific Railroad's (CPR) transportation costs skyrocket.

• In 1908, New York tea importer Thomas Sullivan gives out tea samples in tiny sacks. By 1934, the industry uses 8 million yards of gauze annually to make tea bags.

• Today, Americans consume roughly 80 per cent of their tea iced. During a heat wave at the St. Louis World's Fair, a vendor whose free hot tea samples are refused, dumps ice into the whole lot. A new craze is born.

A Canadian Tea Drinking Survey

Tea Council of Canada (1997 statistics)

Tea Drinking	In British Columbia	For All of Canada
Drink herbal teas	52 per cent	41 per cent
Drink green tea	43 per cent	27 per cent
Drink specialty tea:		
Earl Grey or English Breakfast	56 per cent	34 per cent

A server from Point Ellice displays afternoon tea, to be served in the garden

Taking Tea: Victoria

In Victoria, taking tea is a way of life. Strictly speaking, "High Tea" or "Meat Tea" is the name given to main meal of the day for working and farming people in Great Britain. "High Tea" technically accompanies a full meal. "Low Tea" or "Cream Tea" are the proper names for an afternoon tea break with or without sweets. However, these conventions are not strictly observed in Victoria.

Whatever the accompaniments, the tea service is often made of silver and the cups are of delicate porcelain. Sweets may include assorted finger sandwiches—cucumber or smoked salmon are common—homemade scones with strawberry preserves and thick Jersey or Devonshire cream, berries with Chantilly cream, toasted honey crumpets, dessert pastries, rich lemon tarts, jam tarts, madelaines or tiny cakes.

Cream cakes are served at hotels—never at home. Biscotti goes with coffee, never tea. The pastries are never referred to as "French," though layer cakes are occasionally called "gateaux." Sometimes the sweets and sandwiches are served on a three tiered dish to save room on the tabletop.

Tea is properly taken with milk and/or sugar. Never add cream and lemon together—it curdles horribly. If you desire milk, you take your tea "white." Servers will provide you with a lemon slice for certain types of teas if you wish, but lemon is most appropriate for iced tea, not hot teas.

> *"I don't drink coffee, I 'take' tea, my dear."*
> —Sting,
> English rock singer.

Afternoon Tea in Greater Victoria

Dress codes may be in effect; please inquire. Reservations are always advisable.

Tea Establishment	Location	Reservations (250)
Adrienne's Tea Garden	5325 Cordova Bay Road, Saanich	658-1535
Blethering Place Tea Room	206, 2250 Oak Bay Ave.	598-1413
Empress Hotel Lobby	721 Government Street	384-8111
Four Mile Roadhouse	199 Island Highway, View Royal	479-2514
James Bay Tearoom	332 Menzies Street	382-8282
Oak Bay Beach Hotel	1175 Beach Drive	598-4556
Point Ellice in season	2616 Pleasant Street	380-6506
Point No Point Resort	1505 West Coast Road, Sooke	646-2020
Princess Mary Restaurant	358 Harbour Road	386-3456
The Gatsby Mansion	309 Belleville Street	388-9191
The Olde England Inn	429 Lampson Street	388-2831
Windsor House Tea Room	2540 Windsor Road	595-3135

Special Interest Gardens: Victoria

Carr House and Garden

Emily Carr (1871-1941) was a renowned Canadian painter, writer and potter whose works are featured in prestigious collections around the world. In 1864, Emily's father Richard Carr built this house. Emily writes of her childhood home, "We had a very nice house and a lovely garden..." Carr House and garden have been restored, and admission to the interpretive garden is free. The area is wheelchair accessible.

Location: 207 Government Street .

Geology Garden

An odd little garden, displaying outstanding samples of rocks rather than plants, is of particular interest to those who appreciate the mineral wealth of the five mountain ranges that cover 80 per cent of British Columbia. Some of the rock specimens include sandstone concretions from Denman Island; columnar basalt from Alta Lake; green argillite from Cranbrook; folded quartzite from Duncan Lake; mica schist from Creston; fossil shells from the Upper Pine River; and calcareous tuffa from Clinton. Admission is free and the area is wheelchair accessible.

Location: Front grounds of the Royal British Columbia Museum near the road, at 675 Belleville Street.

Clockwise from top left: Carr House; Geology Garden; Oak Bay Beach Hotel; Heritage cherry tree

Heirloom Black Prince Cherry Tree

This scion of a Black Prince Cherry tree is an historic legacy. Governor James Douglas, the first Governor of British Columbia, planted it in 1854. The original fruit tree was probably brought over from England in a Wardian Case and was a valuable addition to Fort Victoria's kitchen garden. Transplanted in 1997, the cherry tree stands on or near the place where the daughter of Victoria's first doctor is buried. Admission is free and the area is wheelchair accessible.

Location: On the east side grounds of the Royal British Columbia Museum at 675 Belleville Street..

Oak Bay Beach Hotel Garden

The waterfront district of Oak Bay, "behind the Tweed Curtain," is an area dominated by avid gardeners and birders (tweeters). The long legged, purebred whippet is the dog of choice in this area and afternoon tea is a way of life. Indeed, the annual municipal parade is called "The Oak Bay Tea Party." The private gardens at this hotel are well groomed with impressive displays of annuals. Make a reservation for a summer tea on the deck: (250) 598-4556. A map of the Marine Drive Circuit Route, its parks and hilltop stops is available from the Victoria Visitor InfoCentre, (250) 953-2033. Admission to the hotel garden is free and the area is wheelchair accessible.

Location: 1175 Beach Drive.

B.C.'s emerald green waters conceal a different sort of garden.

Undersea Gardens: Victoria

Is the western ocean green because of pollution? The forest industry? Over-fishing? While human activity may influence local waters, the reason for B.C.'s so-called "emerald" waters is the spinning of our planet. As the earth spins, its oceans try to keep up. Create a mental picture. Earth moves in an easterly direction, outrunning or leaving the oceans behind each continent's western

Undersea Gardens

coastlines. As surface water slides westward, it is replaced. Cool, nutrient-laden water wells up from the ocean floor. Known as "upwelling," this phenomenon occurs only along western continental coastlines.

Tiny floating ocean plants called phytoplankton require sunlight and nutrients. In the tropics, sunlight is readily available, but nutrients are scarce. As nutrients deplete, phytoplankton dies. Therefore, tropical waters appear clear. In temperate regions, phytoplankton begins to bloom. as summer days grow longer. Upwelling caused by the earth's rotation continually replenishes the nutrient supply. Therefore, west coastal B.C.'s ocean waters with phytoplankton, a great source of nourishment for all manner of sea life.

Visitors without scuba gear can enjoy a pleasant undersea walk among the plants, plankton and animals of B.C.'s oceanic garden world. This stationary floating garden is home to thousands of Pacific salmon following their life-cycle amid the ruins of a sunken ship. A ghostly array of white anemone wave gently in ocean currents among the world's largest octopi and a variety of underwater vegetation. Admission is charged; the area is not wheelchair accessible. Phone for information: (250) 382-5717.

Location: 490 Belleville Street on the Inner Harbour, opposite the Victoria Parliament Buildings, Victoria.

Hong Kong, Afternoon Tea and Queen Victoria

In 1997, the British rulers of Hong Kong returned it peacefully to mainland China. Police switched uniforms overnight—eliminating all royal insignia. Organizations like the Royal Hong Kong Yacht Club immediately dropped the "Royal." Mailboxes were painted green; every photograph of the Queen was removed; the minutest royal symbol was erased from public buildings.

However, as a tribute to the legacy of the Victorian era, not all royal conventions were dumped. Queen Victoria (the statue) was guaranteed her spot in the park that bears her name, and Hong Kong's Peninsula Hotel continues to serve its famous afternoon high tea and finger sandwiches. Queen Victoria's presence in the park and afternoon high tea in the hotel lobby are the most enduring symbols of Hong Kong's British years.

Victoria Butterfly Gardens: Brentwood Bay

An indoor tropical garden specifically designed for breeding and housing tropical species of butterflies and moths, this facility is one of the largest butterfly conservatories in Canada. The Victoria Butterfly Gardens imports 200 to 250 butterflies each week to ensure that approximately 600 butterflies are flying about the enclosed garden at any time. Butterflies and moths belong to the insect order Lepidoptera. Well-known for their beauty, they act as pollinators for certain plants. The presence of butterflies is an indicator of the reproductive health of our botanical environment. By breeding rare species, butterfly gardens throughout the world claim to ensure that these delicate creatures continue to be part of our fragile ecosystem.

This is a pleasant place to admire some of nature's smaller creatures. The indoor tropical garden is warm and humid, complete with winding cobblestone paths, waterfalls and a running stream. The taller plants shelter the delicate insects, and rocks placed throughout the greenery provide sun-warmed resting sites. Small ponds provide the butterflies with drinking water. The colour and fragrance of the flowers is attractive to both butterflies and humans.

After an optional short video presentation, visitors embark on a self-guided odyssey. Trained guides are available to lead tours, or to answer questions about the buterflies' life cycle. Some of the species on the loose inside the conservatory are the rare Blue Morpho butterfly (Morpho peleides) and the Postman butterfly (Heliconis melpomene). Attracted to your brightly coloured clothing, the little creatures will sometimes land on you. If you sit very quietly on one of the benches near their feeding station, they flutter by in a constant parade. In an area called the "emerging room," rows of chrysalis break open slowly and young butterflies dry their wings before being released into the gardens.

Cameras and video recorders are welcome. The best photographs are possible when school groups are not

It's fun to make friends with a butterfly.

present. Children's shrieks make the butterflies scurry to the uppermost reaches of the dome. Wait 15 minutes after a class has departed and the butterflies will re-emerge. If you visit the dome on a cold day, allow your camera to warm up first, or the lens will fog up in the humid atmosphere. The temperature in the dome is a constant 25°C (80°F). Wedding and birthday parties are welcome. Visit the Nature Gift Shop for theme gifts or educational items. There is an on-site Restaurant, or you can have a boxed lunch made fresh at the delicatessen. Admission is charged, and the area is wheelchair accessible. The Butterfly Gardens are daily from 9 a.m. to dusk. Phone: (250) 652-3822, fax: (250) 652-4683.

Location: On the corner of West Saanich and Keating X Roads, 2 km (1 mile) from The Butchart Gardens, 20 minutes from downtown Victoria and 15 minutes from Swartz Bay Ferry Terminal in Brentwood Bay.

The ritual of weddings as they are practiced in the West today evolved during the Victorian era.

Wedding Gardens: Victoria

It was Queen Victoria herself who inspired the tradition of wearing a white wedding gown. During the Victorian era, white wedding gowns slowly came into vogue.

Before this, a woman tended to buy a black dress for her wedding—one that could be worn on Sundays, and never get soiled. White weddings were a wonderful departure from this austere practice.

The tradition of Saracen (Arabian) brides to wear orange blossoms as an emblem of fecundity at the time of the Crusades was revived in the Victorian era. The flower-language craze made orange blossoms a symbol of marriage. Brides used orange blossoms by the hundreds, sometimes adding a spring of myrtle. Real orange blossoms or hand-fashioned substitutes were employed as a corsage at the throat, at the waist, or in the bridal veil. Flowers were embroidered on undergarments, day dresses and bridal accessories.

The blossoms' whiteness symbolized both chastity and fertility; an orange tree is the most prolific of the fruit trees. The symbol also bears meaning for the groom. It was said that mature, sweet oranges turned bitter by neglect. The groom was thereby warned to pay attention to his wife.

Home was a popular a place to marry. Darkly lit Victorian rooms were decorated lavishly with garden-cut flowers, roses, lilies, potted palms, ferns and similax. Banisters were entwined with cedar boughs and greenery was festooned everywhere. Ribbons, bows and fabric flowers were scattered by the hundreds.

Wedding Gardens in and around Victoria

The following gardens welcome bridal parties and wedding photo shoots with advance notice. The public is welcome to watch the proceedings.

Butterfly Gardens	Brentwood Bay
Crystal Garden	Victoria
Gazebo Restaurant and Gardens	Victoria
Government House	Victoria
Hatley Park Castle Gardens	Sooke
Oak Bay Beach Hotel Garden	Victoria
Playfair Park	Victoria
Sooke Harbour House	Sooke

Vancouver Island Gardens

Vancouver Island is the place to explore secret gardens.

Blessed with the moderating influence of ocean currents and enriched by the resourcefulness of talented island gardeners, the area north of Victoria boasts a number of secret gardens. Scattered along the spine of Vancouver Island, these private gardens are open to the public. One particularly noteworthy stop is the Japanese-style oasis of Larry Aguilar, a raku potter who opens his garden gates to drop-in visitors. His delightfully over-run garden, complete with snapping turtles and hanging baskets, is located near Qualicum Beach at 1180 Ganske, just off the Island Highway. Phone (250) 752-9332. A number of charming private gardens can also be found on the Gulf Islands, particularly during the mid summer festivals on Hornby Island. Near Hoberg on the old San Jospeh Wagon Road is a small paradise called Ronning Gardens, maintained by Julia and Ron Moe. While you are seeking out private gardens, take note of the many highway signs that indicate the studios of potters and craftspeople.

There are many exciting discoveries to be uncovered in the area of commercial nurseries. One particularly enjoyable stop in Port Alberni is "The Old Lady of the Old Roses," a commercial rose-selling establishment with rambling rose gardens.

Vancouver Island is home to several comprehensive arboretums. The Grant Ainscough Arboretum, a 4 ha (10 acre) site in the community of Cedar (near Nanaimo) was opened in 1956. Established for the purpose of studying non-indigenous trees to determine their viability on Vancouver Island, the site also includes a Cone Farm. While it is closed to the public, group tours can be arranged through Harmac Pacific. It is located next to the new highway that leads to the Duke Point Ferry, adjacent to Island Phoenix road. A second arboretum was founded by a lumber baron and world traveller. The main roadway in Masachie Lake Village now has over 240 imported mature trees representing 33 different species. A walk along this line of woody giants is an uplifting experience. Established in the 1940s, it adds a historical dimension to this lakefront community.

Garden Training Programs in British Columbia

Several colleges, public gardens, and post secondary institutions offer horticultural courses and diplomas in landscaping, soil and plant management, garden maintenance or floristry. These programs enhance the professionalism evident in B.C.'s public show gardens. Course details are available directly from the institutions or on the internet.

Floristry or Horticulture Technician	Kwantlen University College	Langley
Horticultural Garden Maintenance and Design	Horticulture Centre of the Pacific	Saanich
Horticulture Certificate Program	Camusun College	Victoria
Horticultural Program	Malaspina College	Nanaimo
Landscape & Horticulture	Capilano College	North Vancouver
Master Gardener Program	VanDusen Botanical Gardens	Vancouver

Left: Tara Bromberger, horticulture student

A Brief History of Global Gardens

Egypt's sacred groves

A Chinese pavilion

Protected medieval garden

- By 3000 BC, Egyptians tend lotus blossoms and cultivate roses. Scenes painted in tombs depict servants tending gardens.
- By 255 BC, Chinese emperors close off huge river valleys to use as hunting grounds. The belief develops that such places hold the secret of immortality.
- By 200 BC, the Romans are "rose maniacs." Slaves tend lotus-filled Water Gardens in natural grottos.
- By 500 AD, monks tend gardens.

- By 700 AD, the Islamic desert world builds water gardens with high walls, fountains and pools.
- By 750 AD in Spain, mosques have courtyard gardens such as the Alhambra.
- By 775 AD, Chinese royal gardens reflect Taoist philosophy.
- During the 1200s in Japan, monks perfect the raked stone garden.
- By 1400 in China, the literati build walled Classical Gardens next to their homes.
- In the late 1400s, Renaissance

Italian engineers build intoxicating water gardens like Villa Lanta and Tivoli, complete with water staircases.
- By 1560, the geometric tapestry hedges of the Elizabethan Knott garden has evolved.
- In the 1630s, Tulips are all the rage in Holland.
- In 1662, mathematician André Le Nôtre designs the French Formal Garden. The Gardens of Versailles, his showpiece, cost $100 million.
- From 1730 onward, Lancelot

Landscape movement

Grand garden style

Cottage garden

A Brief History of Global Gardens

Elizabethan knott garden

Italian water garden

French formal garden

"Capability Brown" perfects the emerging natural landscape movement.
- After 1788, Humphry Repton modifies Brown's landscapes and defines Gardenesque.
- In 1799, Napoleon's wife, Empress Josephine, organizes the first dedicated Rose Garden.
- From 1825 onward, common folks begin to grow flower gardens. The first gardeners' magazines are established.
- Settlers transport precious vegetable seeds to North America and lovingly grow a few

ornamentals. After 1842, the Wardian case revolutionizes botanical shipping.
- In the 1940s, the Victory Garden enables common folks to assist the war effort.
- During the 1970s, gardeners aim to match specific plants to climatic zones. The motto for common folks is "easy care."
- In the 1980s, as increasing numbers of people live above ground level, civic Green Spaces take on new meaning. Once again herbal remedies become

fashionable. In the world's rainforests, a new wave of 20th century plant collecting begins.
- In the 1990s, there is a return to using indigenous plants. The greatest garden innovation of the age is the rediscovery of the wilderness.

Settler's garden

Show garden

A modern green space

Butterfly World: Coombs

The flashes of brightly coloured insects in flight, combined with many blooming tropical plants make Butterfly World a photographer's paradise. At ground level, busy little Chinese quail scurry through the underbrush, painted turtles laze in a pond and songbirds live high in the overhead jungle canopy. The sounds of ever cascading water along with the scents of richly coloured tropicals make a visit to this place a special experience.

Butterflies cluster at a feeding station.

The aesthetic qualities of butterflies have been appreciated for centuries. In Egyptian paintings, medieval manuscripts, and graffiti on modern sidestreet city blocks, butterflies occupy a place in our collective imagination. A Great Plains Native legend states that to have a wish come true, you must capture a butterfly. Whisper your wish to it, and set it free, and the winged messenger will take your request to the Great Spirit.

In many cultures, fluttering butterflies are likened to souls drifting heavenward. Sanskrit weddings in India make frequent reference to butterflies. In America's Appalachia region, a new bride who sees a butterfly on her wedding day knows that she will have good luck throughout her marriage. For this reason, the little creatures are increasingly woven into rites of passage. Butterfly farms or supply houses, independent of the conservatories, now sell individually packaged live butterflies in color coordinated envelopes. As newlyweds emerge after the service,

guests open their envelopes. Masses of butterflies swirl skyward, and the bride and groom proceed under a canopy of coloured wings. Other wedding rituals include butterflies concealed under handbells. When the couple says "I do," butterflies are released in a wonderful flurry of multi-coloured wings and tinkling sounds to announce the joyous news. Sleep-induced butterflies may also be hidden directly within wedding floral arrangements. At random moments during the ceremony, they wake up and emerge from the flowers.

Newspapers and magazines run numerous stories about the new industry of butterfly supply. New York has six butterfly

farms; Texas, Ohio, California, Florida and many other states each have one; Canada, Costa Rica and Mexico are rapidly adding more. Butterfly sales outlets for weddings and celebrations are best accessed through the internet.

Butterfly World, a drop-in butterfly conservatory, is open from April to October. A patio refreshment room is on site. Phone for information: (250)752-1091. Admission is charged, and the area is wheelchair accessible.

Location: In Coombs near Parksville and Qualicum; located 9 km (4 miles) west of Parksville on Highway 4 en route to Cathedral Grove.

British Columbia's Provincial Flower

The western flowering dogwood (*Cornus nuttalli*), also known as the Pacific dogwood, is British Columbia's official provincial flower. A Christian legend claims that a giant specimen the size of an oak tree was chosen long ago as the timber to make the Cross. Jesus, nailed upon it, sensed its distress and promised it that henceforth, its four

blossoms would form a cross; its petals bear rusty nail or blood prints, and its centre resembles a crown of thorns. And so it is today. In the past, dogwood was occasionally made into knitting needles or piano keys, but today its main use is ornamental. Several hybrids with white or pink bi-annual blooms outperform the wild breed in flower size and endurance.

Civic Gardens: Nanaimo

Hailey Rhododendron Grove: Bowen Park

The 350 hybrid plants in this rhododendron grove were a gift from Mrs. Ellen Hailey, a founding member of the Vancouver Rhododendron Society. Visitors enjoy this garden's many surprises: flowers range in size from tiny to colossal, and in colours from soft pink to fiery red. A project is underway to introduce azaleas to the collection and to add cultivars from the 27 rhododendron species native to North America. A student from the Malaspina College Horticultural Program recently catalogued all the species in the grove. Now maintained by the City of Nanaimo and the Nanaimo Rhododendron Society, the irrigated grove is located within a larger 36 ha (90 acre) park. The local Rhododendron Society holds its annual show of rhododendrons and perennials in the Centennial Building in Beban Park on the day before Mother's Day. Admission to the grove is free and the area is wheelchair accessible.

Location: In Bowen Park, Hailey Rhododendron Grove, off Bowen Road and Comox Road, Nanaimo.

> *"Teaching a child not to step on a caterpillar is as important for the child as it is for the caterpillar."*
>
> —Anonymous

Tamagawa Japanese Garden: Malaspina College

Partially funded by the University of Tokyo, this traditional Japanese garden is set in a busy thoroughfare and provides a green oasis for college students. Showing wear from its heavy use during the student year, this somewhat dog-eared garden is planted with green shrubs, sun-loving azaleas, shade-loving rhododendrons, Japanese maples and a flowering cherry tree. The garden contains an ornamental pool once stocked with koi fish. Evident here are the six attributes of Asian gardens: antiquity, artificiality, views, seclusion, spaciousness and water.
- "Antiquity" implies past formulas are followed
- "artificiality" implies nature has been reinterpreted in a satisfying way
- "views" implies there are several physical and mental levels from which to see the garden
- "seclusion" implies a sense of serenity, silence and privacy
- "spaciousness" refers to the manipulating of small areas to make them appear larger
- "water" implies the skillful design of waterfalls, ponds and streams, dry or wet.

Admission is free. Wheelchair accessibility is poor, and there are many stairs.

Location: Malaspina College, Nanaimo. Consult the campus map.

Filburg Lodge and Gardens: Comox

Now a public centre for the arts, this elegant 19th century manor house and its adjoining 3.6 ha (9 acre) estate by the ocean were once the private domain of Robert J. Filburg, president of the Comox Logging Company. In 1929, Master builder William Hagarty supervised the innovative structure. Beams and millwork were hand finished with an adz, and a branching yew tree serves as a unique handrail for the staircase. William Meier, the head gardener, also did the lodge's stonework and included a local Native petroglyph in the wall of the fireplace. The owner intended the gardens to "capture elegance in the wilderness." Its rambling grounds, grape arbors and screeching peacocks do just that. A mature arboretum of stately oaks, London planes, Atlas and Deodar cedars compliment flower beds lining a forest stream. Hundreds of rhododendrons originate from the famous collection of the Greig family; see page 103. Heathers, spring bulbs, flowering shrubs and dwarf conifers thrive in this oceanfront micro-climate. At the bottom of the garden is an impressive totem pole by Coast Salish master carver, Richard Krentz. The lodge is open daily and in early August, vendors and musicians put on an elegant four-day arts festival. Known as one of the best outdoor art sales in the Pacific Northwest, the annual festival in the garden attracts over 25,000 people. For information, phone (250)-334-9242.

A long grape arbour leads to the main house.

Bring a picnic lunch. Admission to the gardens is free; the arts festival is not. The area is mostly wheelchair accessible.

Location: 61 Filburg Road, Comox.

Wildflower Reserves on Vancouver Island

In British Columbia, an order-in-council is all that is required to set aside small reserves of ecological significance. One such area is Honeymoon Bay Wildflower Ecology Reserve where Vancouver Island's largest known concentration of pink fawn lilies is located. Other wildflowers abundant in this area include bleeding hearts, wood violets, white trillium and wild ginger. It is strictly prohibited to pick the flowers. Best viewing is in late April and May, depending on the weather conditions. Admission is free. Wheelchair accessibility is poor.

Location: Honeymoon Bay is found on the south shore of Lake Cowichan at Sutton Creek, 1 km (0.6 miles) past Gordon Bay

A member of the lily-of-the-valley family, white trillium's three petal whorls form lovely solitary flowers.

Park. Ask for specific directions at a local Travel InfoCentre before setting out: (250)756-006.

A second ecological reserve at Rhododendron Lake Reserve near Parksville is best reached with a utility vehicle. In late May and June, this small ecological reserve boasts an abundant stand of Rh. macrophyllum, the wild species native to southern British Columbia. Botanists that believe this reddish strain existed before the last ice age and escaped destruction in valley pockets free from ice; see page 129. Wild rhododendrons are smaller and more weather beaten than their pampered domestic garden cousins. Removal of vegetation is strictly prohibited. Admission is free. Wheelchair accessibility is poor.

Location: Rhododendron Lake Reserve is 7 km (5 miles) south of Parksville on Highway 4, then 14 km (9 miles) along a forestry road. Check with the Parksville Travel InfoCentre for specific directions before setting out: (250) 248-3613.

The Haig-Browns left a legacy of thoughtful conservation.

Today Ms. Marci Prior maintains the Haig-Brown gardens. In keeping with Ann's strict guidelines, limited improvements are made.

From 1936 to 1976, Roderick made his living as a writer. Written in an easy, conversational style, strongly argued and based on sound research, his writing is still respected. The Western Angler (1939) remains the definitive work on western fly fishing. Always seeking to be practical philosophers, the Haig-Browns sought to answers to the great ecological questions of our time: What is the place of humanity in nature? How are we to live along with nature without destroying its legacy?

Jeff Mason and a team of trained interpreters offer natural history tours and school programs. Contact phone numbers are: (250) 286-6646; fax (250) 286-6694. Admission fees are by donation; guided tours require a set fee. The area is mostly wheelchair accessible.

Location: 2250 Campbell River Road or Highway 28, 10 minutes from Campbell River.

Haig-Brown House and Gardens: Campbell River

Roderick Haig-Brown (d. 1976), writer, conservationist and fly fisherman, influenced a generation of conservationists. Both he and his wife Ann, devoted their lives to ecological causes and were pivotal in raising the first alarm about the emerging plight of the salmon. Today, the home they called "Above Tide" is known as The Haig-Brown House Education Centre. Its eight riverfront hectares (20 acres) provide an excellent venue for a bed and breakfast stay, a seminar or a simple drop-in visit. Of the total acreage, 1 ha (2.5 acres) are cultivated flower gardens. The Haig-Browns also enhanced their estate with more than 30 varieties of ornamental trees, both native and exotic. Blossoms are at their best in May and June, and the arboretum is the focal point until late September. The surrounding woodlands are interlaced with streams and trails and are home to migrating birds and salmon.

> *"Any given generation... can have only a lease, not ownership, of the earth."*
>
> —Roderick Haig-Brown

Arboretums in Vancouver

Arboretum	University of British Columbia Campus	88 different trees; Persian ironwood, Kentucky coffee tree, tree-of-heaven
Riverview Arboretum	500 Lougheed Highway, Coquitlam; kiosk on site	3000 trees; pin oaks, Tasmanian cedars
Simon Fraser Arboretum	Simon Fraser University Grounds	Various trees
The Crescent	Shaughnessy District	47 different trees
Vancouver Parks Board Tree Walk	7 blocks, Alma and 11th Ave, Trutch and 13th	Various trees; booklet available: (604) 257-8600

Greater Vancouver Gardens

Little Mountain

Rockwood Arboretum

Arboretums: Southwestern B.C.

Little Mountain Arboretum

During its establishment in the 1940s, this arboretum's founders boasted that it would someday grow every species of woody plant that could survive year round in Vancouver. Perhaps this braggadocio was a little far reaching, but the result of their efforts is a mountainside of colourful contrasts with a wondrous collection of trees and shrubs. One notable specimen is the pyramid-shaped monkey puzzle (also called monkey pine or Chilean pine), a tree that grows up to 30 m (90 feet) high with rope-like branches and very sharp needles. At one time, its finely grained wood was used for interior woodwork, but because wild monkey puzzles grow at high altitudes in South America's Andes, very little wood is exported today. Wander freely around the mountainside. Wheelchair accessibility is fair.

Location: The entrance is on 33rd and Cambie Street in Queen Elizabeth Park, Vancouver.

Rockwood Arboretum

Established in 1935 when the Rockwood Lodge was a resort for vacationers arriving on Union steamships, this mature arboretum is located on the resort's grounds. You may want to search out the star attractions: Photinia, European beech, windmill palm, Stewart golden cypress, thread branch cypress, Chilean monkey Puzzle and Sequoia gigantica. Warm seasons can be spectacular when the foliage is full, while winter seasons provide an interesting look at the structure of woody plants. Today, the Lodge is famous for its festival in the garden, an annual three-day Sunshine Coast Festival of the Written Arts that takes place in August; (604) 885-9631, 800-565-9631. Renowned writers from across Canada come to lecture and read at this event. Admission is free to the arboretum; there is a fee for the Festival in the garden. Wheelchair accessibility is fair.

Location: Shorncliffe and Cowrie Street in Sechelt, on the Sunshine Coast.

Left: Riverview Arboretum. "The wonder is that we can see these trees and not wonder more."—Ralph Waldo Emerson, 1850

Arthur Erickson's Garden: Vancouver

In 1996, various philanthropists from Montreal to Vancouver established a financial plan to rescue the home and garden of Canada's foremost architect, Arthur Erickson. At stake was Erickson's West Point Grey corner lot.

In 1957, Erickson purchased a property and expanded the house on its grounds. With the assistance of talented student Werner Forster, he developed an Asian-inspired garden. Using marble, he created a watery landscape of ponds and greenery, a contemplative enclosure he later claimed was one of the keys to his creative process. Indeed, an impressive portfolio evolved: Simon Fraser University; the MacMillan Bloedel Building; B.C. Law Courts; The University of Lethbridge; The Canadian Chancery, Washington DC; the Bank of Canada and the Museum of Anthropology.

Erickson's personal garden incorporates water lilies,

"Show me your garden and I shall tell you who you are."
—Alfred Austin, English poet, 1910

bulrushes, wild iris and families of lively frogs. The latter give rise to complaints from neighbours, who say the incessant croaking interferes with their own creative concentration. Noise aside, the Erickson's design lets the site speak for itself. The American Society of Architectural Historians visited the garden in 1995 and were awestruck by its "magical poetic spirit." The garden was featured in the TV "Northwest Gardens" as one of the major influences in Northwest garden style.

Make advance arrangements to view the garden with the Arthur Erickson House and Garden Foundation, Suite 709, 700 West Pender Street, Vancouver, B.C., V6C 1G8. Phone (604) 444-6894/224-1558. Admission is charged and the area is wheelchair accessible.

Location: 4195 West 14th Avenue, Vancouver.

West Coast Cedar

Once useful to coastal aboriginal peoples, Western red cedar (*Thuja placata*) and yellow Alaska cedar (*Chamaecyparis nootkatensis*) are common west coast trees. From them, native people derived materials for shelter, clothing, tools and transportation. Women who collected the cedar bark and roots saw the tree as a helpful sister and begged its forgiveness as they worked. Strips of bark were beaten into baskets, rope and mats, or woven into clothing and rain hats. Shredded

Totem at Capilano Suspension Bridge

bark was used for bandages, washcloths and towels. The most slender branches were fashioned into fish traps and ropes, while baskets and cradles were fashioned from the roots. Men felled trees by burning through the trunks. By boiling out the trunk's interior and widening it with sticks, they manufactured large dugout canoes capable of long ocean voyages. Trunks were also fashioned into shingles for roofs, planks for longhouses and full-sized totem poles.

Richmond Nature Park

B.C. Native Plant Gardens: Greater Vancouver

An unprecedented effort to restore and retain native vegetation is taking root in Greater Vancouver. A government-funded program, "Naturescape B.C.," encourages a new approach to selective planting that is more natural and saves more water than traditional methods. Phone 800-387-9853.

Its objective is to use native plants in municipal parks, in public show gardens and along boulevards as well as in private citizens' backyards and patios. The municipality of Port Moody has adopted the Naturescape program; Burnaby and Richmond have instituted policies favouring native vegetation; Vancouver is considering the policy, and other municipalities are expected to follow.

Indigenous animals have a close relationship with native plants. In many cases, imported plant species do not provide animals with habitat, nesting material, protection or food. Although it rains amply in Vancouver, the city's water reservoirs drain quickly during dry spells. Surprisingly, Vancouver's gardeners endure summer water restrictions. Native plants, which are better equipped to survive local weather conditions and require little watering, are in demand. Besides promoting the program to municipalities, Naturescape B.C. makes presentations at garden shows, plant sales and community events.

Although it is the first of its kind in Canada, this program borrows elements from similar projects in Washington and other parts of the U.S. Native plant expert Wilf Nicholls of the U.B.C. Botanical Garden says that while one need not plant excessive amounts of native species, they do have the advantage of attracting butterflies and hummingbirds. He notes local nurseries are responding to increasing demands, while at the same time, "the variety and sheer number of native plants are increasing." He predicts a gradual shift away from British traditions to more natural methods of gardening.

If the major garden trends of the past 500 years remain constant, the current movement toward the "natural" is merely the forerunner of an outstanding new innovation in garden design; see page 156.

B.C. Native Plant Gardens: Greater Vancouver

City of Vancouver Waterwise Demonstration Garden	2150 Maple Street (at 6th Avenue), Vancouver	(604) 873-7350 (604) 255-5719
Bear Creek Park, Nature Walk	13750-88th Avenue, Surrey	(604) 501-5050
Delta Compost Demonstration Garden	7046 Brown Street (off River Road), Tilbury Industrial Park, Delta	(604) 946-9828
Museum of Anthropology, Native Plant Garden	U.B.C. Campus, Vancouver	(604) 822-3825
Native Education Centre, Mount Pleasant	285 East 5th Avenue (at Scotia Street), Vancouver	(604) 873-3761
Park and Tilford Gardens, Native Plant Garden	440, 333 Brooksbank Avenue, North Vancouver	(604) 984-8200
Richmond Nature Park	11851 Westminster Hwy, Richmond	(604) 273-7015
U.B.C. Botanical Garden	6804 SW Marine Drive (at 16th Avenue), Vancouver	(604) 822-9666
Wildlife Rescue Habitat Demonstration Garden	5216 Glencairn Drive, Burnaby	(604) 526-7275

Burnaby's Haunted Garden

Century Gardens are rumoured to receive visits from as-yet-unidentified lugubrious spirits. Many speculate that these spirits originate from the sad past of the Fairacres Mansion, now serving as the Burnaby Art Gallery. In 1909, the mansion's gardens were created by Mrs. Ceperley, the wife of a Vancouver real estate tycoon. Her dying wish, that the proceeds from the sale of her estate be used to build a children's playground in Stanley Park, was never honoured. She is said to haunt the third floor of the house and possibly the grounds, along with

Burnaby Art Gallery

several waif-like children. Manifesting themselves either as vapourous vortexes or vague sounds, the children were

apparently victimized in the 1950s when an unorthodox cult, run by an abusive bigamist and convicted extortionist, used the mansion as a residential school. Staff at the art gallery, repair labourers, night security personnel and investigative journalists have variously reported nudges, cold feelings, audible footsteps, missing objects and transparent sightings.

B.C.'s three other haunted gardens (two are in Victoria and one is in Kelowna), are also listed in this book.

Meaningful Flower for Canadians: the Poppy

One of the scenes most commonly associated with Canada is Lake Louise and its beds of Icelandic Poppies—*Papaver nudicaule*. Since

Poppies at Lake Louise

the heyday of Railway Demonstration Gardens, these alpine flowers have graced the beds of C.P.'s Chateau Lake Louise and inspired countless generations of visitors.

Due to the literary efforts of a young Canadian doctor, Lieutenant John McCrae, poppies are also a flower of war remembrance. McCrae's poem "In Flanders Fields" links the European roadside red poppy, P. rhoeas, with war's death toll. "In Flanders fields the poppies blow, Between the crosses, row

on row...To you from failing hands we throw, The torch, be yours to hold it high. If ye break faith with us who die We shall not sleep, though poppies grow In Flanders fields." First published in England's *Punch* magazine in December 1915, it came to symbolize war's ultimate sacrifice. It is comforting to learn that the young doctor had the satisfaction of knowing his poem was a success. Today, the poppy continues to be an official part of Remembrance Day ceremonies in the United States, France, Britain, Canada and other Commonwealth countries.

Rhododendron Festival in Burnaby

Jeanne Mitchell, Chair of the Burnaby Rhododendron Gardens Society, stands near the hybrid Burnaby Centennial and a publication of the American Rhododendron Society in which this prize-winning hybrid is recognized. Century Gardens' Rhododendron Festival is held in early May.

Admission is free or by donation. For information, phone Burnaby Rhododendron Gardens Society: (604) 205-3004.

Century Gardens rhododendrons are at their best in early May.

Century Gardens: Burnaby

Century Gardens, founded by the Burnaby Centennial Committee to commemorate the 1967 Centennial of Confederation in Canada, is located on a sunny, sloping hillside overlooking a pleasant urban lake. The 1.5 ha (3.7 acre) garden occupies the grounds of an imposing Tudor-style mansion. Once known as Fairacres, it is now used as Burnaby's Art Gallery.

Circular pathways are bordered with displays of rhododendrons, azaleas and roses. The perimeter is surrounded by mature evergreens. In season, hundreds of rhododendrons with names like cosmopolitan pink, moon wax, and

sugared almond, create a kaleidoscopic effect. On the adjoining lake, preening mallards, buffleheads, goldeneyes and teals jostle each other for handouts from picnic makers.

The genus Rhododendron grows luxuriantly throughout the Pacific Northwest. Easily propagated, relatively free of insect problems, craving acid soils with a ph between 4.5 and 6.5, rhododendrons thrive along the west coast. Back in 1966, the municipality of Burnaby claimed this floral wonder as their official civic emblem. Later, in celebration of their city's 1992 Centennial, the Burnaby Beautification Committee sponsored a competition to develop their own varieties of the flower. Winning the award was a hybrid cross, aptly named Burnaby Centennial. Developed by Dr. and Mrs. Finley, it is located in the garden near the bronze plaque. Admission is free, and the area is wheelchair: accessible.

Location: 6344 Deer Lake Avenue, Deer Lake Park, Burnaby.

Burnaby Centennial, a hybrid cross, is one of many distinctive blooms produced by local breeders.

Gardens and Parks with Waterfowl in Greater Vancouver

These gardens and parks include lakes or very large ponds where waterfowl including Canada geese, wood ducks, mallards and teal are abundant.

Century Gardens and Deer Lake	Burnaby
Friendship Gardens	New Westminster
Little Mountain Arboretum	Vancouver
Minnekhada	Coquitlam
Nitobe Memorial Garden	U.B.C. Campus, Vancouver
Stanley Park	Vancouver
VanDusen Botanical Garden	Vancouver

Ultimate Balance: Yin and Yang

Taoist philosophy has greatly influenced the development of Asian garden style. Concerned with tranquillity of mind and the improvement of temperament, the bustle of city life was once considered to be ill-suited to those seeking self-discipline. Therefore, a fervent Taoist considered it virtuous to search for an isolated wilderness areas where he could lead the life of a hermit. Such places existed only in remote mountain valleys. Here, they found little or no sound or movement. Over time such hermitages were deemed unsuitable because the winds were too strong; the air, though fresh, was often foggy; obtaining food was difficult; and unattended diseases caused premature death. Furthermore, they were in constant danger of being attacked by wild animals. For these reasons, it was said, many Tao hermits failed to reach their destiny—a life of transcendental bliss.

Taoist elders developed alternative strategies: private gardens were designed to imitate remote mountain valleys and to eliminate their negative elements. Arts, meditation, reflection and poetry were practiced in such gardens, and the techniques of martial art were developed to gain good health and to resist animal attacks.

The ensuing Taoist philosophies of yin and yang or life forces in balance are present today in all Asian gardens. The feminine or yin is soft, receptive, intuitive, inward, sensitive, delicate, emotional and nurturing. The masculine or yang is outward, hard, thrusting, logical, strong, rational, rough and loud. These two principles are assumed to be in eternal opposition. When carefully manipulated, they can be placed in dynamic balance to achieve harmony. When this happens, chi—a powerful living breath, much like a refreshing flow of air—is liberated.

In gardens in which yin and yang are balanced properly, light is balanced with dark; open spaces alternate with enclosed ones; cold shadows give way to sunlit places; exposed views vie with protected areas; vertical elements contrast with horizontal; details are set against simplicity; manmade competes with natural. Rugged, hard objects are balanced by soft, flowing elements. For example, a shard of

Yin and yang can be experienced as light and dark, gnarled and straight, simple and complex, tension and release.

rock might stand silhouetted against a soft, feathery bamboo stand. The rock is considered yang: hard, unmoving, stubborn, "masculine," while the bamboo is considered yin: receptive, yielding, forgiving, "feminine." The deliberate arrangement of complimentary opposites creates alternating tensions and releases that are said to help viewers transcend ordinary levels of awareness and to achieve inner wisdom.

Asian Gardens in Greater Vancouver

The following are Asian gardens, have sub-gardens illustrating Asian design, or have large areas dedicated to Asian plants.

Dr. Sun Yat-Sen Classical Chinese Garden	Chinatown, Vancouver
Fantasy Garden World	Richmond
Friendship Gardens	City Hall, New Westminster
Friendship Garden	Hope, see Fraser Valley
Kuno Garden	Garry Point Park, Richmond
Minter Gardens	Rosedale (Bridal Falls)
Nitobe Memorial Garden	U.B.C. Campus, Vancouver
Kwan Yin Buddhist Garden	Richmond
Park and Tilford Gardens	North Vancouver
U.B.C. Botanical Garden	U.B.C. Campus, Vancouver
VanDusen Botanical Garden	Vancouver

A Brief History of Chinese Garden Styles

Dating back to 500 BC, China has the oldest continuous tradition of garden design in the world.

Imperial Hunting Parks

As early as 220 BC, powerful Chinese emperors sectioned off huge hunting parks for their exclusive use. There, they collected rare animals, exotic birds and unusual waterfowl from the remotest corners of their empires.

Imperial hunting parks

Among these mysterious misty mountains and cascading waterfalls, a poignant legend grew: immortality could be found here. Painters and poets sought communion with dragon spirits; philosophers told of vanishing hermits; warlords aggrandized their conquests by re-enacting battles. Enormous pagoda-style palaces built on these reserves were strategically located to overlook the shrouded, cloud-covered hills. Surrounding each palace were private walled gardens—forbidden to common folk. Today, no Imperial hunting parks remain.

Monastic Stone Gardens

"Nature lovers were so captivated by this spot that they forgot to go home."—Chang Lun describing a monastery garden in China, 547 AD. For thousands of years, Chinese monks cultivated austere gardens of reverently arranged rocks. These still collages were said to last 1,000 years. Certain limestone rocks—contorted Taihu boulders—were revered and named. Monastic gardens are best viewed in the pouring rain or during a snowy winter day.

Monastic garden

Scholar's garden

Scholar's Gardens

Evolving in the 1400s, government bureaucrats' private walled gardens became places of entertainment. Pavilion rooms, tiled walls and lattice windows are tightly arranged so one experiences nature as a series of still images: water-eroded limestones (Taihu rocks); murky, jade green waters; naked branches against the sky; coloured pebbles underfoot; a container with a single bonsai. The purpose of these gardens is to "nourish the heart": to escape the unrest of the world and enter into a delightful fantasy of landscape painting, poetry and tai chi.

Tea Gardens

From the 1200s to the 1700s, small social gardens were prominent both within China and along busy cargo routes where Asian traders and their camel caravans moved silk, tea and porcelain. Within China, tea gardens were located near religious temples or on the grounds of prominent merchants' palatial homes. They contained a few lacquered tables and chairs, important stones, a few plantings of bamboo, landscape paintings and calligraphy on scrolls, and men engaged in business transactions while sipping the celestial beverage—tea. Today's modern coffee houses are rough equivalents of traditional Chinese Tea Gardens.

Tea garden

Dr. Sun Yat-Sen Classical Chinese Garden: Vancouver

Modeled on a courtyard-centred Scholar's Garden such as those constructed by wealthy literati in the Garden City of Suzhou, this recreated 15th century Ming dynasty garden is named after Dr. Sun Yat-Sen (1866-1925). Two other major gardens also carry the name of this frequent visitor to the west coast and hero of the 1911 Chinese revolution. One is a public garden in central Beijing, and the second is a Chinese hall in Overfelt Gardens in San Jose, California. The $6.5 million dedicated to build Vancouver's Sun Yat-Sen Garden was funded by private donations, three levels of Canadian government and The People's Republic of China. See page 32.

In March of 1985, 52 Chinese experts under the direction of master garden architects Wang Zu-Xin and Fen Xiao Lin arrived in Vancouver. Fresh from constructing Astor Garden Court at the Metropolitan Museum in New York, they were armed with a secret recipe for Chinese lacquer. Throughout the year, exotic shipments arrived: camphor wood rafters, special limestone Taihu rocks, Gingko-wood screens, rare Nan wood pillars and roof tiles fired in imperial kilns. Because Taoist philosophy is the metaphor for all Chinese garden construction, these skillful architects designed the walls, pools, pavilions, rocks, courtyards, lattice screens and paving in the proper symbolic fashion. All elements are positioned to create channels for ch'i, a powerful life breath said to be present in all things.

As visitors enter the small courtyard, potted metasequoia sets the tone for the gloomy area. From there, visitors emerge into a stream of light and the garden unrolls like a scroll from right to left. The sound of dripping water emanates from the False Mountain of the T'ing, where a chalky, jade green pool is home to several box turtles, Koi and goldfish.

High tiled walls separate the garden from the noise of Chinatown, and the roof eaves transform rain droplets into beaded curtains of water. Upright, porous Taihu limestone rocks, imported from Lake Tai, resemble garden sculptures. A double covered walkway gently curves . This is said to discourage sha qi—unfavourable energy. The high walls are punctuated with 36 lattice-patterned leak windows. Each opening allows scenery from the adjacent public park to "leak" inside. Pathways, embedded with pebbles and pottery shards, are a gentle reminder that all things ultimately return to the earth. Passing through the Water Pavilion with its intricate grillwork, the visitor arrives at the Moon Gate Lookout. From here, one is meant to stop and ponder the entire Garden as it opens up to the secluded Scholar's Courtyard. Here, the master of the house would listen to music, drink tea, compose poetry, practice calligraphy and create freehand brush paintings. Behind each of his windows is a meditation plant: a bamboo, a pine tree and a winter flowering plum. Banquets were sometimes held in these courtyards

> *"I have banished all worldly care from my garden; it is a clean and open spot."*
>
> —Hsieh Ling-yin, 410 AD

Christopher Chin, Wu-Shu World Champion, puts on one of many Garden demonstrations.

Properly called a T'ing, this garden pavilion is set on False Mountain.

and an important part of the event was the composition of tanka poetry. This practice originated with Wang Xizhi, a Chinese calligrapher, and was a popular pastime.

Volunteer guides are on hand to explain the Garden's symbolism. Hot Chinese tea is available. While in the Garden, search for the Secret Grotto, admire a pine bough, discover examples of yin and yang. If the 0.1 ha (0.3 acre) and adjoining 0.4 ha (1 acre) public park seem small, you are moving too fast. Many special events are held here: lectures, brush-art displays, photography exhibits, chrysanthemum shows, bonsai displays, musical evenings and martial art demonstrations. Phone for information: (604) 662-3207. Admission is charged, and the area is mostly wheelchair accessible.

Location: 578 Carrall Street, Vancouver.

Chinese Language of Flowers

Though much of the biological richness in today's western gardens originated from botanical specimens collected in China and Tibet about 100 years ago, Chinese custom permits few such plants in their own formal gardens. Stones are the basic elements of design. Scholars study, paint and compose poetry about the few authorized garden plants.

Permitted Plant	Inherent Virtues	Symbolism
Bamboo	longevity	lasting friendship
Conifers	tenacity, persistence	great dragons of old age
Chrysanthemum	naturalness	the courage to sacrifice
Narcissus	regeneration	resistance to boorishness
Dogwood	strength	aversion to evil
Lotus blossom	nobility	spiritual purity, paradise
Orchid	wonder	the perfect personality
Peach blossom	freshness	new life
Pine	hardiness	strength of character
Plum blossoms	pleasure of life	the return of spring, hope
Tree peony	kingship	wealth
Willow	grace	the feminine spirit

The dogwood's virtue is its strength.

77

Three Garden Styles

Japanese

Chinese

English

	Japanese Stroll Garden	Chinese Classical Garden	English Country Garden
Architectural elements	• arched bridge • teahouse (optional) • stone lanterns • waterways	• Walls • pavilions • leak windows • moon gate	All are optional • arbour • low gate • fence
Attitude toward nature	Nature bids humans emulate a celestial landscape	Nature is balanced and should be contemplated	Rejoice in the abundant beauty of the earth
Best seasons	• Spring, autumn	• Summer, winter	• Summer, spring
Energies in the garden	• kami, soothing, good energies	• 'chi(qi) ; yin and yang	• links to the land
Flowers	• a few camellias, irises, azaleas	• a few authorized blossoms	• abundant blooms
Garden life	• Koi fish and turtles • waterfowl, ducks	• Koi fish and turtles • nightingale	• bees and birds • rabbits
Intended use	• peaceful walking • escape from routine • a formal tea ceremony	• studying, writing • entertaining • tai chi or qui gong	• resting in a hammock • working • dining, eating & teas
Landscape forms	• contrived undulations • stone groupings • running streams & ponds • raked white sand bed	• balance of yin and yang • enclosed courtyards • stones, pebbles • still green pond	• lush flower beds • plants set in harmony
Location	• within a city park • within a monastery	• at a rich man's home • on palace grounds	• surrounding a home
Mythical garden creatures	• Kappa, water sprite	• Guardian stones	• fairies, gnomes & elves
Sounds	• silence • ducks	• dripping water • Chinese music	• buzzing bees • chirping birds
Striking features	• arched bridge • stone lanterns	• Taihu rocks • Pavilions, T'ing	• floral borders
Water courses	• reflective pools	• jade green pool	• lily pond

"Its liquor is like the sweetest dew from Heaven." Tea Master Lu Yu, 8th Century

A Brief History of Chinese Tea

• According to Chinese legend, Emperor Shen Nung was sitting beneath a tree about 4,000 years ago while his servant was boiling drinking water. A leaf from a nearby camellia bush dropped into the water and Emperor Nung decided to try the ensuing brew. The rest is history.

> *"Rather go without salt for three days than without tea for a single day."*
>
> —A Chinese Proverb

• By the end of the Tang Dynasty (618-906 BC), tea had become China's national drink.

• By 1610, the demand for spices, Chinese crockery and tea drove the Dutch East India Company to unprecedented feats of exploration, competition and commerce.

• As part of ancient Chinese wedding traditions, the boy's family presented betrothal gifts of money, tea, bridal cakes, poultry, sweetmeats, sugar, wine and tobacco to the girls' family. These gifts were known as *cha-li*, "tea presents."

• From the 11th to the 15th centuries, tea houses grew up along the Silk Road and at public gathering places throughout China.

• In the 12th century, a Buddhist priest exported the tea tradition to Japan, where it developed elaborate variations.

• At present, although 40 countries have commercial tea plantations, China accounts for about 18 per cent of world exports.

• In addition to black tea, China produces five other principal types: Green, Oolong, Scented, Compressed and, the rarest of all, White.

The Ten Noble Flowers of China

The meaning of these flowers was first defined during the Sung Dynasty:

Distinguished friend

Lotus blossom	sacred friend	Gardenia	meditative friend
Crab apple blossom	distinguished friend	Cassia blossoms	hermetic friend
Chrysanthemum	excellent friend	Kerria (yellow rose)	poetic friend
Peony	lustrous friend	Jasmine	elegant friend
Plum blossom	pure friend	Daphne	exceptional friend

Chinese Tea Houses

Chinese Tea House	Location	Phone (604)
Bubble World Enterprises Tea House	7974 Granville Street, Vancouver	263-6031
Little Tea House	2260 President Plaza, 8181 Cambie Road, Richmond	231-5822
Ten Lee Hong Enterprises	500 Main Street, Chinatown, Vancouver	689-7598
Ten Ren Tea and Ginseng Co. (Vancouver) Ltd.	550 Main Street , Chinatown, Vancouver	684-1566
The Best Tea House	120 Central Square, Hazelbridge Way, Richmond, just south of Aberdeen Centre	303-7623

The Christian Garden

Fantasy Garden World: Richmond

Fantasy Garden World was transformed in the 1980s by the Honourable Bill VanderZalm while he was premier of British Columbia. Prior to his political career, Mr. VanderZalm was a tulip vendor and garden nursery owner. To demonstrate his family's love of horticulture, Dutch roots and Christian faith, he and his wife expanded an existing garden.

Today, the garden hosts a steady stream of brides and grooms. Vancouver Castle—a replica of Holland's Coevorden leads visitors through an Olde World Village. Tulips and bulbs are exquisite in the spring, and the Rose Garden is a popular destination in the summer. The Biblical Garden features vignettes from the life of Christ. Banquets are held in The Glass Conservatory, The Rose Ballroom or the smaller patio rooms. Admission is charged; wheelchair access is good. Phone (604) 277-7777.

Location: 10800 No. 5 Road, corner of Steveston Highway and No. 5 Road, Richmond.

"Every man's life is a fairy tale written by God's fingers."
- Hans Christian Anderson

The Lesson of the Rose

"I can complain because rosebushes have thorns, Or rejoice because the thorn bush has a rose."

—Anonymous

The chimera, a creature derived from a lion and a dragon, is a protective figure.

Kuan Yin Buddhist Temple Garden: Richmond

For centuries, Zen Buddhist masters have recognized the therapeutic effects of natural spaces on the spirit. As the ancient practice of Buddhism spread from India through China and Japan, each of these nations developed a theory of garden construction. The placement of rocks and water

In addition to the garden itself, the temple courtyard and its shrines are open to respectful viewing.

in a particular way was thought to promote inner enlightenment.

Next to a palatial Buddhist temple in Richmond, a 0.4 ha (1 acre) Buddhist garden, with its shrines, tiled courtyards and golden statues, is open to the public. The garden's central feature, the Siddhartha Gotama Pool, is named after the great Buddha himself. At his birth, fragrant flowers are said to have drifted down from

the sky after which time he received enlightenment while sitting under a Banyan tree. A penjing (bonsai) collection and pots of feathery bamboo adorn the courtyard. The continuous chanting of a melodic mantra from concealed loudspeakers evokes the Asian origins of this garden.

Buddhist philosophy states, "the awakening of one's enlightened mind is beyond linguistic description. Truth has existence beyond words."

Such reasoning makes the task of describing this Buddhist garden a daunting one. The best solution is to experience it yourself, preferably on a sunny Sunday afternoon in summer. In addition, visitors can arrange to view the Buddhist temple, museum and library. Garden visitors are not pressured to take part in religious activities. Those not participating in the service are asked to stand quietly to one side. Please ask the worshippers' permission before taking photographs. Modest clothing is appropriate. Special events include religious observances, tea ceremonies, flower arranging and bonsai demonstrations. Guided tours are held from time to time. Phone for information, (604) 274-2822. Admission is free; the area is not wheelchair accessible.

Location: 9160 Steveston Highway, between No. 3 and No. 4 Roads, Richmond.

Bonsai or Penjing Displays in Vancouver

A bonsai (called a penjing in the Chinese tradition) is a miniature tree encouraged to grow in a particular way. Its shape is maintained by confining it to a small pot, pinching out top growth, pruning its roots, and wrapping wire around its limbs. The art began in China about 1,000 years ago, then spread to Japan and beyond. Like a pet, a bonsai must

be cared for each day of its life.
• Dr. Sun Yat-Sen Classical Chinese Gardens Vancouver
• Kuan Yin Buddhist Temple Richmond
• Nitobe Memorial Garden, Vancouver
• Minter Gardens, Rosedale
• U.B.C. Botanical Garden, Vancouver
• VanDusen Botanical Garden, Vancouver

> *"There is nothing useless in nature; not even uselessness itself."*
>
> —Zen proverb

A Brief History of Japanese Garden Styles

Long ago, Japan's national cult, known as Shinto or the Way of the Gods, associated the notion of beauty with certain "perfect" scenic land forms. Among them are the classic cone-shaped Mount Fuji and the mounded Pineclad Islands of Matsushima Bay. These shapes inspired the first Japanese gardens. When envoys began to visit China in 500 AD, the Chinese style became a second major influence.

Basic Garden or Niwa

The Basic Garden consists of mounded beds of mosses, grasses, stones, and shrubs emulating the Pineclad Islands. Plants are trained to form gourd-like mounds symbolizing happiness. The joyful emotion of seeing cherry trees burst into bloom is said to match the elation that results from drinking sake.

Natural Garden

The Natural Garden, sometimes called a Moss Garden, is defined by the damp, dark feeling typically experienced at the motionless end of winding waterscapes. Concentrations of deep greenery, irises, and mosses make this the wettest, darkest place in a garden.

Stroll Garden

The Stroll Garden's defining elements include stone lanterns, subdued plantings, winding paths, waterfalls, bridges arching over ponds, and carefully designed rock layouts. While these gardens appear natural, every centimetre has been carefully manipulated to create a dream-like appearance. Since the 1620s, these gardens mimicked or "borrowed" the characteristic mountain and valley shapes of larger

Basic garden

Natural garden

Stroll garden

Tea garden

Zen garden

landscapes. In these gardens, visitors escape the tiresome rituals of everyday life.

Tea Garden

First developed in the 1600s, the Tea Garden is a deeply spiritual place designed to break one's connections with the outside world. The rojia or path consists of irregularly laid stepping blocks leading to a nakakkurgui-mon or "diving-in-gate." The hut itself has simple paper walls and is never oriented toward a scenic viewpoint. Nothing must distract guests from the tea itself.

Zen Garden

The Zen Garden, a variation of the Chinese Monastic Stone Garden, was developed in Japan by 1000 AD. Sometimes called a Sand and Stone Garden, it is always surrounded by a wall or a fence. The stones, sand and gravel are arranged in wave-like patterns. In monasteries, monks create the designs. In public gardens however, visitors are sometimes invited to use a wooden rake to carve the sand into symbolic ocean waves.

> *"Now ....*
> *I am in Japan."*
> —Japan's Crown Prince, 1980, on visiting Nitobe Memorial Garden

"Unlike the western glorification of the vertical dimension, Japanese gardens celebrate the horizontal or ground plane."
—Arthur Erickson, architect

"Yesterday's lovely flower is but a dream today."—Japanese Proverb

Nitobe Memorial Garden: Vancouver

In 1960, Japanese landscape architect Kannosuke Mori of Chiba University, began the monumental task of creating an authentic Japanese garden outside Japan. By combining imported azaleas, irises and trees from Japan with local trees and shrubs, Mori has achieved the finest creation of his career. The seemingly effortless grounding of a man-made garden in the surrounding landscape was a hallmark of Mori's work. Nitobe Memorial Garden demonstrates his intuitive feel for site-specific design and his belief that Zen evolves in response to a site's physical characteristics. In 1992, the garden was renovated under the supervision of landscape architect and Zen monk, Shunmyo Toshiaki Mansuno from Yokohama. He was ably assisted by the illustrious Shinichi Sano from Kyoto. Sano's input was invaluable, as his family has passed gardening skills down from father to son for 18 generations.

The resulting garden is dedicated to the memory of Dr. Inazo Nitobe (1862-1933), a scholar and early advocate of world peace. In his tireless lifetime efforts to build a "bridge across the Pacific," he visited Victoria, Vancouver and, during his last days, Banff. He passed away in Victoria.

The metaphors surrounding Japanese landscape architecture have evolved over the thousands of years. Like its kindred gardens in Japan, this one is meant to foster *zanzen*, an enlightened serenity of mind. The entrance, a ceremonial grass-thatched gateway punctuating the Nightingale Fence (an earthen wall), leads to a glorious vista of flowering cherries (in season). The gaze is directed across the pond to a shelter and the Tenth Bridge, made of earth and logs. It is one of six water crossings in the garden.

Nitobe's Quiet Tea Garden

Thick vegetation hides the enchanting Nitobe Tea Garden. Its stepping-stone path is carpeted with moss and the green coolness reminds us to stop and shed our preoccupations. Near the Tea House is a tsukaubai or "water-holding stone" (shown here). To use it, the participant must bend low, a position of humility and ceremonial cleansing. When the tiny tea house is open, an ikebana (flower arrangement) and

painted scroll welcome visitors to formal tea ceremonies. The scroll is specially painted for each ceremony and contains words of wisdom such as "Deru kugi wa utareru." Translation: "The nail that sticks out will get hammered in." Whether you are strolling casually through the Tea Garden or waiting to be summoned by the tea host, silence and calm are appreciated.

Kuno Garden

Located on a dry streambed, Kuno Garden, commemorates the 100th anniversary of the first Japanese immigrant's arrival to Canada. Hailing from Wakayama Prefecture, Mr. Gihei Kuno led a group of compatriots here and befriended many of the locals. The 0.1 ha (0.25 acre) garden was dedicated to his memory in 1988. Admission is free, and the area wheelchair accessible.

Location: Entrance to Garry Point Park, End of Chatham and 7th Avenue, Richmond.

Within the pond, Koi fish flash mysteriously and nearby, stone outcroppings floating in balanced arrangements remind us of mountains, lakes, and valleys. The idea of abstraction or *skakkei* in landscaping—reducing nature to its simplest form and using that symbol to evoke the larger whole, is an integral part of Japanese garden design.

Near the noisy waterfall,

the pebble beach surrounding the Nitobe Memorial Lantern is carefully maintained. Across the Yatsu-shaski Bridge, Japanese irises flourish in the damp environment. There are meant to be few flowers in Asian gardens, as they tend to distract one's attention from deep meditation. To enjoy the beauty of this garden, slow your pace.

Friendship Garden

[The word] *Visit comes from visum, "to see"...It and vision stand related. To visit means to see, not to talk, but to take notice, to take note, to actively engage the eye....*
—John Stilgoe, author, describing the gardens of Japan.

Celebrating the garden traditions of New Westminster's

Japanese sister city, Moriguchi, the Friendship Gardens are located on a one ha (2.5 acre) site with flowering cherry trees and a busy, duck-filled pond. Admission is free and the area is partially wheelchair accessible.

Location: adjacent to the New Westminster City Hall, Royal Avenue.

Information: Nitobe Memorial Garden

Type	Formal, Japanese Stroll and Tea Garden, administered by the University of British Columbia
Size	One ha (2.5 acres)
Time allotment	90 minutes to 2 hours
Open	10 a.m. to 6 p.m.; may vary in summer
Year round	No, closes weekends in winter.
Best seasons	Spring (flowering cherries) , summer, autumn (maple leaves)
Sub gardens	Stroll Garden, Tea Garden, Nightingale Fence, flowering cherries, Tenth Bridge, 6 water crossings, koi fish pond, Nitobe Memorial Lantern , 14 stone lanterns, Yatsu-shaski Bridge
Additional features	Tea House (always closed, except for ceremonies)
Events	Periodic Japanese Tea Ceremonies in summer; extra charge
Admission charged	Yes. Discount in effect if combining with admission to U.B.C. Botanical Garden. As a public service there are some free days; phone ahead.
Wheelchair access	Mostly accessible with a few rough patches
Guided tours	By arrangement only
Telephone	(604) 822-6038, (604) 822-9666
Location	University of British Columbia Campus, across from the Museum of Anthropology, N.W. Marine Drive, Vancouver
Nearby attractions	U.B.C. Botanical Garden

Left: The Japanese proverb, "A fallen blossom does not return to the branch," reminds us to take advantage of the summer in order to see Nitobe at its best.

Cha-no-yu: the Japanese Tea Ceremony

1. Master Kouchi's graduates

2. Hostess Yukiko begins

3. Indoor fire pit for winter

1. Under the direction of tea master, Akira Kouchi, graduate members of Vancouver's Omote-san-ke Doko-kai Tea School perform a ceremony in their private garden especially for readers of this garden book. The master explains this Zen art involves no more than preparing, serving and washing a cup of green tea. The goal is that the ceremony be conducted in the most polite, graceful and charming manner possible. This beautiful ritual requires years of training and practice.

2. Our hostess, Ms. Yukiko Basley, assembles her utensils. In this ceremony, an earthenware tea bowl, portable charcoal brazier, green tea container, spout pot for wash water, water ladle, tiny scoop (*chachaku*), bamboo whisk (*chasen*), and gauze are made ready. The tea host's duties are to execute an intricate series of movements. Our duties as guests are to observe the presentation in silence, enjoy the tea and admire the tea bowl, the garden and the hostess.

3. Throughout the year, tea ceremonies are performed in different settings. On the day of the New Year, a thick tea is shared from a single bowl and the day before

spring equinox, a sunrise ceremony featuring pink flowers is held. In April, the ceremony is performed under the cherry blossoms. Summer ceremonies take place at the seashore or high in the mountains. As the weather cools, these rituals take place indoors. In November, new tatami mats are laid down for December, an especially busy tea season. No two tea ceremonies are identical; each ceremony is individually choreographed to evoke coolness in summer and coziness in winter.

4. In this view, Yukiko ritually unfolds her napkin or chakin. She cleans the utensils and prewarms the tea bowl. Well before the ceremony, our tea master

7. Serving the guests

chooses appropriate earthenware tea bowls to be used on this day. Antique tea bowls are extremely valuable and no two tea bowls are identical. For indoor ceremonies, the tea master prepares seasonal flowers (*ikebana*) and paints a small scroll for guests to enjoy. A scroll message might read: "Surrounded by a forest of enemy spears, enter deeply and learn to use your mind as a shield."

5. Our host puts *macha*, powdered green tea, into the warmed bowl and adds near-boiling water. Zempo, an ancient tea master, was more interested in the tea bowl than the tea itself: "Indeed…a gold brazier…is splendid, but it does not make any impression on the mind. But if

8. Cleaning the utensils

Cha-no-yu: the Japanese Tea Ceremony

4. Chakin unfolding

5. Green tea

6. Making a froth

the rough earthenware…is used, it is the heart which will be deeply satisfied."

6. The delicate tea is whipped until frothy with a bamboo whisk. Each motion of the hand, each facial expression and each body posture is practiced to achieve economy and grace of movement. First-time guests at a tea ceremony are often too nervous to appreciate the appeal of drinking tea in an atmosphere requiring so much etiquette. The key is to relax and enjoy the serenity of the ceremony.

7. A helper, Ms. Reiko Sato, serves our representative guest, Ms. Etsuko Taylor. She takes the tea bowl in both hands, and turns the cup a quarter turn clockwise,

twice. She aligns the design away from her lips, bows slightly, tastes it, wipes the cup where her lips touched it, turns the cup counter-clockwise, and drinks. She politely makes a slight slurping sound when tasting the last sip. Then she compliments the host on the look and feel of the tea bowl and the calmness of the setting.

8. Each guest is served, one at a time. Then, the tea bowls are ceremoniously returned to the host. As seen here, our host begins a complex ritual of cleaning the utensils. Reflected in each ceremony are the qualities of *wa, kei, sei,* and *jyaku. Wa* implies harmony between all things; *kei* involves respect to all; *sei* is extreme cleanliness (syn-

onymous with a clear mind); *jyaku* is a state of calmness arising from the beautiful simplicity of the ceremony.

9. The bowls are cleaned with hot water and the utensils with cold water. Each is placed in harmonious juxtaposition with the other pieces. One well-known 15th century tea master Takeno Jo-o, said that each ceremony must be performed as though it were the participants' only chance to experience perfection.

10. Our host ceremoniously pours out the waste water, replaces the hot water for the next use and removes her utensils. Her last action is to show us the tea container (*cha-ki*) and the tea scoop. We admire them appreciatively. The tea ceremony depicted in these photographs took place over a period of 30 minutes. This school's alumni meet once a week and choreograph tea ceremonies in various settings. These students especially like garden ceremonies because they do not have to sit on their feet. Graduates get used to it, but novices have been known to tip over when their feet go to sleep.

9. Perfect cleanliness

10. Replacing the water

Rainforest Walks in Greater Vancouver

Garden visitors often appreciate the chance to see a West Coast rainforest. Here are a few sites where the trails are easy to walk and the forests are mature.

Capilano River Regional Park	Rainforest Trails	North Vancouver
Cypress Mountain Park	Yew Lake Nature Walk	West Vancouver
Lighthouse Park	Rainforest Walk	West Vancouver
Lynn Canyon Park	Rainforest Trails	North Vancouver
Mount Seymour Park	Goldie Lake Trail Walk	North Vancouver
Pacific Spirit Park	Swordfern Trail Walk	Vancouver
Seymour Demonstration Forest	Rainforest Trail	North Vancouver

Garden Tours in Vancouver

Allayne Cook, retired Head Gardener

With the increasing popularity of gardening as a hobby, there has been a renewed interest in visiting nurseries and Show Gardens around the world. A number of tour operators now sponsor fully escorted tours to England's and New Zealand's Great Gardens. The Vancouver Parks Board, (604) 257-8400, coordinates occasional local garden tours; the Vancouver School Board Continuing Education Department, (604) 733-1893, offers courses in gardening and Show Garden tours. Other school districts' Continuing Education departments do the same. Hospital Auxiliary Groups occasionally organize private garden tours in season. These can be discovered in the "What's On" columns of local and regional newspapers in. The Saturday Vancouver Sun features a column by Steve Whysall, who covers major garden events.

Knowledgeable English or German-speaking guides who can help visitors plan their itineraries, for B.C. garden tours are available through West Coast Garden Friends, (604) 463-0890 or (604) 463-2486. Clubs, groups and organizations requiring custom 3 to 6-hour local tours may car pool or hire a charter coach. Longer tours are available on request.

Once a hunting lodge, this property's gardens and adjoining marshes are one of the few Western Canadian examples of a pleasance.

Minnekhada Regional Park: Coquitlam

A pleasance or pleasure ground is typically attached to a mansion-estate. Often used as hunting grounds, pleasances are forerunners to the practice of setting aside protected wilderness areas as parks.

As early as 728 AD, returning crusaders were impressed by Arabic walled compounds set up for sporting purposes. In 1086, William the Conqueror had gardens and orchards built on 14 of his 75 hunting manors. The grounds were stocked with deer; mill ponds were constructed for waterfowl and fish; forests were planted. In 1110 AD, Henry I built hunting lodges on the grounds of Woodstock in Oxfordshire. Because many guests came simply to watch the deer or to fish, the concept arose of "a pleasing sight" or a place to "park."

While there are many pleasances in Europe, the settlement patterns in western Canada would seem to preclude such places. However, there are a few exceptions. Minnekhada was originally built in the 1930s as a hunting estate by Eric Hamber, Lieutenant Governor of British Columbia. The regal atmosphere of the lodge's Scottish Tudor architecture was the setting of many elegant parties

Today, 219 ha (540 acres) of marsh and forest are home to beavers, muskrats, waterfowl, bullfrogs, deer and bears. Fanning outward from the private gardens are picnic grounds and flower beds. Minnekhada Regional Park is run by the Greater Vancouver Regional District. The lodge is open the first Sunday of each month, except January, from 1 to 4 p.m. No hunting is allowed. Admission is free, and the area is wheelchair accessible.

Location: Quarry Road, Coquitlam. From Lougheed Highway, turn north on Coast Meridian Road, drive 2.5 km, then turn right onto Apel Drive. Signs will direct you to the lodge.

Additional Pleasances in British Columbia

Pleasances are defined by concentric outward layering: large house, courtyard, private gardens, glen, great park, lake or seashore.

Century Gardens and Deer Lake	Burnaby
Filberg Lodge and grounds	Comox
Guisachan Heritage Park (modified)	Kelowna
Haig-Brown House and Kingfisher Creek	Campbell River
Hatley Park Castle and Grounds	Victoria

Park and Tilford Gardens: North Vancouver

Designed in 1967 by landscape architects Justice and Webb, this show garden was originally created by Park and Tilford (P&T) Distilleries Ltd. (now Schenley Canada Inc.) as a community beautification project. It was an immediate success and although it hosted up to 300,000 visitors a year, it closed in 1984 following the relocation of the distillery. For several years, it fell into disrepair until corporate donations rescued it in December, 1988.

Today, P&T Gardens features a series of themed outdoor rooms, each with a distinct design. The Native Garden winds through a lush undergrowth of ferns, trillium and huckleberry. Its tall cedars hide the fact that, behind the blue-tiled Moon Gate is a western interpretation of an Asian Garden. In it, bamboo, bonsai and Japanese maples surround a pond filled with water irises. Plants with silver leaves and milk-coloured flowers growing under a canopy of spring flowering magnolias make the White Garden an interesting spot. The Rose Garden, well supplied with Canadian-bred roses, is formally laid out with a water fountain, a long pergola covered in pink Queen Elizabeths, and a wrought iron gazebo. There, an enormous, Wisteria blooms in May while Clematis and Lonicera ramble up brick pillars and fences. Richly textured vegetation and a captivating waterfall enhance the strong features of the Rock Garden, while the circular Herb Garden is a fragrant

The Handkerchief or Dove Tree

In 1898, an English horticulturalist travelled to China to find a distant relative of the flowering dogwood. Father Armand David, a French missionary, stationed in China, reported that "flowers… hung from the branches like handkerchiefs and fluttered like doves in the wind." Kew Gardens was eager to propagate a living specimen.

Kew Gardens' Ernest H. Wilson's subsequent expeditions to northwest China and Tibet not only yielded 17,000 seeds from the sought-after tree, but over a thousand different plants now common in gardens everywhere. Travelling by mule train to remote mountain areas, surviving armed insurrections, peasant revolts, hazardous gorge crossings, rock slides and shattered limbs, his botanical forays between 1898 and 1910 are directly responsible for such garden familiars as primroses, magnolias, poppies, various roses and rhododendrons. His most famous acquisition was the *Lilium regale*, the white trumpeted lily associated with Easter.

Three magnificent specimens of the unusual *Davida involucrata*, with its drooping, tissue-like flowers, are found in Vancouver. It blooms in May: Greig Rhododendron Garden, Stanley Park, Vancouver; Park and Tilford Gardens, North Vancouver; VanDusen Botanical Garden, Vancouver.

The red bridge is said to bring good fortune to all who cross it. According to feng shui, red is a celebratory, energizing colour commonly associated with wealth. The Moon Gate is a symbol of perfection.

arrangement of thyme, mints, bergamot, fennel, culinary and medicinal herbs and poppies. The Colonade Garden features a Spanish style pergola, over 70 m (200 feet) in length, heavily laden with grape vines and hanging fuchsia baskets and bordered with magnolias, rhododendrons and perky Hosta. Small birds twitter in the aviary.

The "Garden Room" concept, first conceived in England during the 1930s, is the basis for P and T's sub-gardens. A Wisteria covered Gazebo overlooks the Rose Garden.

Park and Tilford Gardens

Type	Private non-profit teaching and display garden, open to the public and wedding parties
Size	One ha (2.5 acres)
Time allotment	45 minutes to 1 hour
Open	9:30 a.m. to dusk
Year round	Yes
Best seasons	Summer
Sub gardens	B.C. Native Garden, Moon Gate, Display Garden, White Garden, Rose Garden, Rock Garden, Herb Garden, The Colonade Garden, small aviary, Handkerchief Tree
Additional features	Coffee houses nearby
Events	None for the public at this time; wedding photography shoots are common. The Christmas Lights Festival is canceled.
Admission charged	None; adjacent parking is also free
Wheelchair access	Mostly accessible
Guided tours	By arrangement for groups of 10 or more
Telephone	(604) 984-8200, fax (604) 984-6099
Location	440–333 Brooksbank Ave., southwest corner of the shopping centre, North Vancouver, B.C.
Nearby attractions	Capilano Suspension Bridge, a walk in B.C.'s rain forest

A Brief History of the Search for the Perfect Rose

Hybrid tea roses, along with Floribunda and Grandiflora roses, have been the leading cultivated roses for less than a century. During this relatively short period, their predecessors became mere historical footnotes. However, there is a surge of renewed interest in finicky but beautiful Old Roses. Rosarians visit run-down gardens, cemeteries, churches and town sites to identify the roses growing there. Many have sentimental attachments to old roses, and the subject of identification causes many heart-felt debates. Descriptions from old catalogues, magazines and books published when the cultivars were current are helpful in resolving such issues. Several local horticultural societies now collect data about rose populations in their respective areas.

All ancient roses descend from one of two rose groups growing wild in the Northern Hemisphere: the European-Mediterranean or the Asian variety. The original European type blooms once each year, while Asian roses bloom continuously. In medieval Europe, Damasks, Albas and Gallicas were used for Christian festivals, in medicinal gardens and in the distillation of rose essence. In the 1600s, when Dutch merchant fleets began to trade tulips, Netherlands tulip breeders experimented with the ten known European rose cultivars to create about 100 varieties. In 1800, French Empress Josephine assembled these varieties into a single garden and encouraged a new

"... There is no time to them. There is simply the rose. It is perfect in every moment of its existence."
—Ralph Waldo Emerson, 1850

hybridization program. French breeders Dupont and Descemet developed several hundred new cultivars.

Although little is known about Chinese rose breeding, historians have discovered that by 1750, "the four stud Chinas" had been developed. Two were China roses: one pink, one red; two were tea roses: one blush, one pale yellow. Although they blossomed continuously, they were not hardy. Once they were introduced to Europe, they were expertly crossed and re-crossed and repeat-blooming hybrids began to appear. In the 1840s, the Victorian era's favourite was born—a multi-hued group called hybrid perpetuals. Meanwhile,

on Reunion Island in the Indian Ocean, a cross between a China and a Damask perpetual resulted in the wildly successful bourbon rose. After 1850, rose competitions and the floral-arranging business flourished. The rose assumed a new status as a decorative plant rather than a mere garden flower. The breeder's goal at the time was to produce a hardy, brightly hued, high centered yellow rose. There were light yellow blooms among the tea roses, but they faded over time. In the 1890s, Pernet Ducher's experimentation in crossing hybrid perpetuals with teas produced not only a successful yellow rose, but the genetic basis for the hybrid tea roses so popular today. While this rose dominated rose gardens from the 1920s onward, many new rose cultivars are being developed. Since most of the garden roses cultivated in the last 100 years are founded on only 10 Chinese diploid species, 95 per cent of the genus has yet to be cultivated.

During the 60-year-long experimentation flurry culminating in hybrid teas, a number of intermediate breeds were stabilized. These old cultivars are attracting renewed interest.. One of the reasons for the popularity of Yesterday's Roses is their glorious fragrance; much of this characteristic was sacrificed in favour of tight buds, neatly unfurling, centres and hardiness.

Yesterday's Roses

Name	Appearance	Examples
Gallica Roses; bred from old "French Rose," R. gallica	Stocky plants, open blossoms, showy stamens, hues from light rose to pink	D'Aguesseau, Camaieux, Tuscany, Versicolor
Alba Roses; from medieval castle gardens, 1200s	Large shrubs, fragrant, white or light pink blossoms, few-flowered clusters	Great Maiden's Blush, Semiplena, Jeanne d'Arc, Konigin von Danemark
Damask Roses; via Crusaders from Damascus, Syria, 1254	Upright, arching canes, grayish-green leaves, large fragrant blossoms, white to deep pink	Ville de Bruxelles, Celsiana, Mme. Hardy, Mme. Zoetmans, Kazanlyk
Centifolia Roses; featured in Dutch masters' paintings	4 to 5 feet high, leafy, lush, fragrant, nodding blossoms white to deep red	Common Centifolia, Bullata, Des Peintres, La Noblesse, Tour de Malakoff, Unica
Sweetbriar Rose or Rubiginosa	Tall-growing, foliage wafts a green-apple scent, single pink or white blossoms	Clementine, Hebe's Lip, Lord Penzance, Amy Robsart, Greenmantle
Setigera Roses; hardy native of the American prairies	Tough, hardy climbers	Baltimore Belle, Gem of the Prairies, Eva Corinne, Mrs. F.F. Prentiss, Doubloons
Multiflora Roses; associated with the Old American West	Climbers, ramblers	Veilchenblau, Bleu Magenta, Hiawatha, Caroubier, Ghislaine de Feligonde
Damask Perpetual Roses; unusual old repeat bloomers	Stocky, decorative bushes, double, fragrant blossoms, white, pink deep red	Tous les Mois, Bifera, Jacques Cartier, Yolande d'Aragon, Portland Rose, Rose du Roi
China Roses; continuous blooms	Bushy, twiggy plants, irregular in outline, deep red, maroon, pink and white, poor tolerance to cold	Cramoisi Superieur, Parsons' Pink China, Eugene de Beauharnais, Archiduc Charles, Arethusa, Viridiflora the green rose
Tea Roses: scent of the choicest tea.	Spiraling form, unfurling rose bud, all colours, delicate hues	Anna Olivier, Maman Cochet, Safrano, Comtesse de Labarthe
Bourbon Roses; 1830s roses, presently very popular	Arching growth, deep red, pink, blush, white	Souvenir de la Malmaison, Reine Victoria, Louise Odier, Gloire des Rosomanes
Noisette Roses; 1850s roses	Large-growing shrubs, clusters of lightly fragrant blossoms, many colours	Gloire de Dijon, Desprez a Fleur Jaune, Bougainville, Chromatella' Solfatare
Hybrid China, Hybrid Bourbon, Hybrid Noisette Roses	Extreme profusion and beautiful, fragrant flowers, blooms once a season	George IV, Belle de Crecy, Duchesse de Montebello, Triomphe de Laffay
Hybrid Perpetual Roses; 1820s	Big "cabbage" blossoms at the top of long, arching canes, fragrant, prone to fungal diseases	Baronne Prevost, Reine des Violettes, Victor Verdier, Charles Lefevre, Jules Margottin, American Beauty
Old Hybrid Tea Roses; intermediate breeder, 1860s	delicate, nods on the stem; blushing muted colours	Grace Darling, Captain Christy, Mme. Lacharme, Antonine Verdier, Jean Sisley, Julius Finger
Rugosa Roses; from the thorny Japanese rose R. rugosa	Wine red, white, red, pink and purple, glossy green leaves, splendid hips and flowers	Roseraie de l'Hay, Fimbriata, Mme. Alvarez del Campo, New Century, Comte d'Epremesnil, Rose Apples
Polyantha Roses; from Japan around 1862	Immense clusters of small blossoms, dwarfish, compact bushes, multi-hued	Mlle. Cecile Brunner, Perle d'Or, Rita Sammons, Lady Ann Kidwell, Mignonette

The Royal Visit of the Queen Mum

Long before Diana, Princess of Wales set the popular press afire in the 1980s, there was a member of Britain's royal family who caused a stir wherever she went. Poised and fashionable, Lady Elizabeth Bowes-Lyon married well. Even before her husband Prince Albert ascended the throne unexpectedly to become King George VI, Lady Elizabeth exhibited an elegance that caught the eye of the Commonwealth. As she approaches her 100th birthday, the mother of the reigning monarch is known affectionately as the "Queen Mum." The two "Elizabeths" have periodically caused confusion. However, there was no confusion on May 29, 1939 when King George VI, father of the present queen, and Queen Elizabeth the Queen Mother made a brief royal visit to Vancouver. The city burst with excitement. Thousands of people waited hours for a glimpse of the cavalcade before the royal couple attended a civic luncheon at the Hotel Vancouver. The room was so heavily festooned with West Coast greenery, it was a wonder anyone could see through the indoor forest of cedar boughs. During her Vancouver stopover, the well-travelled queen made an endearing statement: "This seems to me the place to live."

The royal couple's daughter was only 9 months old at the time of her mother's visit. Vancouver's mayor and Council named a park, not for baby "Lilibet," but for the Queen Mum.

The Queen Mother is a noted garden aficionado. Her keen interest in gardening has resulted in a lifetime of styling at four

Queen Elizabeth, along with His Worship, Mayor J. Lyle Telford, takes the Seaforth's Royal Salute during her 1939 visit to Vancouver. Below: The Queen Mother, age 87, in her gardens at Royal Lodge.

royal private gardens in Great Britain: Royal Lodge, Windsor; Clarence House, London; Castle of Mey, Caithness; and Birkhall, Deeside. In keeping with the tradition of several English queens she is a devoted garden designer, plant collector, and botanist.

The Royal Lodge grounds of the Great Park, a pleasance at Windsor Castle, is still a place for riding, shooting, fishing, farming, deer breeding and forestry. HRH Queen Elizabeth reconditioned it in the 1970s, adding acres of flowering bushes and dozens of spring flower beds.

Clarence House is the Queen Mother's London home. The gardens here have been revamped several times in the last 50 years, and now feature romantic flower beds in all shades of blue, her favourite colour. At the remote and windswept Castle of Mey in Scotland, set in a windswept remoteness, she has experimented with windbreaks, hardy roses, kitchen gardens and masses of bedding plants. At Birkhall, her holiday home on the river Dee, she has enhanced the forests, added kitchen gardens, and had the initials ER cut into the turf on the steps of the new terraces. Each of her four gardens has been designed to reflect its location, the climate and the season that Her Majesty spends there.

Vancouver's Queen Elizabeth Park, arboretum, Bloedel Conservatory, rose gardens and Quarry Gardens are privileged to have a garden-loving royal patron.

"Give a man secure possession of a bleak rock, and he will turn it into a garden…" —Arthur Young

Queen Elizabeth Park and Quarry Gardens: Vancouver

Queen Elizabeth Park is noted for its mountainside arboretum, rose garden, and panoramic views of downtown Vancouver and the North Shore mountains beyond. Nearly 6 million annual visitors, including a significant number of wedding parties, marvel at the Quarry Gardens on the 170 m (510 foot) summit of Little Mountain.

In the early 1900s, Vancouver's first roadways were graveled with crushed rock quarried from this mountain. In 1929, the City briefly used the resulting hollows as holding reservoirs for drinking water. Later, the B.C. Tulip Association pressed the city to transform the ugly scars into two sunken gardens to emulate The Butchart Gardens. City Parks transformed 52 ha (130 acres) of Little Mountain's hillsides into a civic arboretum, where native and imported species were planted. Park Board Deputy Superintendent and influential garden enthusiast Bill Livingstone designed, completed and unveiled Quarry Gardens in the early 1960s. A smaller, dry garden commemorates the City's 75th Anniversary.

The Bloedel Floral Conservatory is located next to the quarries. Nearby are the Seasons in the Park Restaurant and Coffee Shop (604) 874-8008; a Pitch and Putt Golf Course (604) 874-8336; and a rose garden. Many bridal parties circulate in and out of the garden on Saturday afternoons in the summer from 12 p.m. to late afternoon. Admission is free, and the area is mostly wheelchair accessible.

Location: 33rd and Cambie Street, Vancouver, B.C.

Henry Moore

"I would rather have a piece of my sculpture put in a landscape, than in or on the most beautiful building I know," declared renowned sculptor Henry Moore (1898 -1986) in 1951. Today, his remarkable works stand both in public parks and on private rural estates around the world. "Sculpture is an art of the open air. Daylight, sunlight, is necessary to it, and for me its best setting and

complement is nature."

Perhaps the most influential public sculptor of this century, Moore created an original and modern lexicon of sculptural form that reflects the human condition. Drawing on his studies of classical, pre-Columbian and African abstractions, he created a series of organic, rounded shapes. Also well known are his seated, standing or reclining figures. "I would like to think my sculpture has a force, a strength, a life, a vitality from inside it, so you have a sense that the form is pressing…trying to burst or to give off the strength…." Moore's works are found on elegant properties throughout Europe, Australia, New Zealand, Israel, Japan, the United States and eastern Canada. Moore's work, entitled Knife Edge—Two Piece, is pictured here. It is found near the Bloedel Floral Conservatory in Queen Elizabeth Park, Vancouver.

The Bloedel Floral Conservatory

Found within Queen Elizabeth Park, this 23 m (70 foot.) triodetic dome encloses three botanical habitats: tropical, rain forest and desert. Growing in a controlled environment, palm trees soar overhead. Their fronds provide a private jungle for more than a hundred brightly coloured birds. Near the bubbling stream, quails dart among exotic bromeliads, banana trees and tongue-thrusting orchids. Golden-coloured koi fish seem perpetually huddled for feeding. With grating caws, the 14-year-old free-flying "Charlie," a peachy-white Moluccan Indonesian cockatoo, stands on his perch. Mostly, he ignores the crowds who are drawn to his antics. Four of his somewhat quieter Amazonian macaw friends also make their home here: a green wing, (predominantly bright scarlet in colour) and his blue and gold companions. Regardless of the weather, the moist, warm tropical interior carries the sweet smell of white gardenias and stirs up a poignant longing for tropical islands.

Lumber industrialist Prentice Bloedel, more frequently associated with The Bloedel Reserve and gardens on Bainbridge Island in the nearby state of Washington, contributed $1.25 million to the construction of this attraction in 1971. Information about Vancouver's facility is available from the Bloedel Floral Conservatory, (604) 257-8584. Admission is charged, and the area is wheelchair accessible.

Location: 33rd and Cambie Street, Vancouver.

"To be overpowered by the fragrance of flowers is a delectable form of defeat."—Beverly Nichols, English writer

Official Flowers of the Provinces and Territories: Canada

Northwest Territories	Mountain avens
Yukon	Purple fireweed
British Columbia	Dogwood
Alberta	Wild rose
Saskatchewan	Wild prairie lily
Manitoba	Crocus
Ontario	Trillium
Quebec	White lily
New Brunswick	Blue violet
Nova Scotia	Mayflower
Prince Edward Island	Lady's slipper
Newfoundland	Pitcher plant

The Riverview Horticultural Centre Society is dedicated to saving an arboretum with hundreds of exotic trees now approaching their centenary.
Below:"Botany John" Davidson, sparked a flurry of plant identification in B.C. in 1911.

Riverview Lands Arboretum: Coquitlam

In 1904, 405 ha (1000 acres) of land, known as Colony Farm, was purchased on the outskirts of Vancouver for a new mental hospital. Soon to be known as the Riverview Lands, and under the direction of B.C.'s provincial secretary, Dr. Henry Esson Young, teams of patients cleared the woods, did the blasting, dyked the boggy lowlands, pulled stumps, plowed the land, laid a road, erected greenhouses and built a nursery. Until the early 1960s, patients planted, maintained, harvested and processed large annual crops of fruits and vegetables.

Canada's first botanical garden was established at Queen's College in Kingston in 1861; the first in western Canada was the prestigious Essondale Botanical Garden, founded in 1904 on the Riverview Lands.

As the University of British Columbia (U.B.C.) came into being around 1911, "Botany John" Davidson, a university-fellow from Aberdeen Scotland, was appointed to organize botanical specimens. With enthusiastic public support, Davidson initiated a province-wide program asking field surveyors, school children and housewives to collect plants. Some 500 specimens a month began to arrive in his tiny Vancouver office. All were classified and many were grown. Davidson's herbarium soon stretched throughout the Riverview Lands and included ornamental trees from around the world. This quickly expanded into a formal arboretum with some 60 species of trees, some of which arrived from remote regions of B.C. by pack horse. Tirelessly, Davidson organized plant-hunting expeditions along rivers, valleys and high alpine meadows.

By 1916, Riverview's botanical collections were transported to U.B.C. at Point Grey, where Davidson became a professor.

Today, the massive mental health facility is almost empty and the Riverview Lands and its century of botanical work are under redevelopment pressures. Hundreds of silver maples, tulip trees, majestic oaks and elms stand in stately maturity. Periodic guided tours are held; phone (604) 290-9910. Private tours are available through Cable Baker, (604) 433-9910. Admission is free, and the area is wheelchair accessible.

Location: Enter at 500 Lougheed Highway, Coquitlam; follow the signs.

Rose Gardens: Greater Vancouver

Burnaby Centennial Rose Garden

Set atop a mountain with panoramic views of Indian Arm, this rose garden is especially enchanting on sunny summer days. Two full-sized B.C. totem compliment the Japanese collection of Ainu poles from the island of Hokkaido. Bring a picnic and spend an afternoon among the totems and the roses. Admission is free, and the area is wheelchair accessible, although there are many hills.

Location: Summit of Burnaby Mountain, 100 Centennial Way, Burnaby.

Centennial Rose Garden

"My love is like a red, red rose that's newly sprung in June." Robert Burns, Scottish Poet (1759-1790). The Fraser Pacific Rose Society echoes this sentiment with a sumptuous display of ruby red roses that climb over the entrance gate. More than 900 additional multi-coloured rose bushes are maintained by this active society, and a major rose show is open to the public in late June. Admission is free, and the area is wheelchair accessible.

Location: 624 Poirier Street, Coquitlam.

Park and Tilford Rose Garden

When was the last time you stopped to smell the roses? The best time to take a whiff is mid-morning, when the sun has just reached the roses. The fragrance is most intense when the bud is half open. Experiment for yourself among the 280 rose plants in

Clockwise from top left: Burnaby Centennial Rose Garden; Coquitlam Centennial Rose Garden; Park and Tilford Rose Garden; Queen Elizabeth Park Rose Garden

bloom at this organically maintained rose garden. A number of Canadian-bred roses from the Explorer and Parkland series are at their height in June and July as is an exceptional specimen of "Queen Elizabeth" that is trained to climb an arbour. Admission is free, and the area is wheelchair accessible.

Location: 440, 333 Brooksbank

Ave. on the southwest corner of the shopping centre, North Vancouver.

Queen Elizabeth Park Rose Garden

Where should a person look for the grandiflora pink rose known as "Queen Elizabeth"? In Queen Elizabeth Park, of course. This rose garden is located along the mountainside. If you are on the summit at the Quarry Gardens, you are in the wrong place. Follow the roadside markers to the rose garden. Citizens have been clamouring to sustain this spot despite impending municipal budget cuts. Admission is free, and the area is difficult to travel by wheelchair.

Location: Little Mountain at 33rd Avenue at Cambie Street, Vancouver.

Vancouver Rose Societies
Fraser Pacific Rose Society
625 Cottonwood Ave., Coquitlam BC V3J 2S5
(604) 931-5120

Vancouver Rose Society
c/o VanDusen Botanical Garden
(604) 936-1514

Hybrid tea, "Timothy Eaton"

Morden's Parkland "Jens Mons"

Cascade Coral

A Brief History of Canadian-bred Roses

The long, cold winter that grips much of the country sets the parameters for Canada's rose breeders. Delicate Canadian-bred roses such as the pink hybrid tea, Timothy Eaton, are rare indeed. A few Western nurseries, notably H.M. Eddie and Sons, did much early hybridizing. In 1961, Ottawa 's Agriculture and Agri-Food Canada (AAFC) crossed a Japanese rambling rose with a number of winter-hardy *Rosa rugosas*, to produce the "Canadian Explorer Series." In 1986, the program was transferred to Quebec; in 1994, funding was severely curtailed. Through innovative financing, the AAFC facility in Morden, Manitoba continues to introduce new cultivars such as the "Parkland Rose Series." Regrettably, there is little emphasis on Canadian-bred roses in B.C.'s public rose gardens; a few exceptions are noted below.

In 1997, Morden AAFC biologists accompanied American rose researchers on a plant-collecting trip to China. Newly collected rose germplasm is placed in a repository in Nan-jing. After quarantine at the USDA Plant Germplasm Inspection Station, they become available to Canadian researchers.

The Canadian Red Cross Society introduced a new rose, in 1995 in honour of their 100th anniversary. Called Hope for Humanity, it is a "blood" red rose with a needle-sharp bud and a drop of white. In 1997, Grand Forks, B.C. introduced Super Cascade Coral, a miniature patio-container rose developed by Brad Jalbert, a skilled rosarian from Langley, B.C.

Where to See Canadian Roses

Roses	On Display	To Purchase
Parkland Series: Rosa arkansana	Park and Tilford Gardens, North Vancouver	Hortico Nurseries, Ontario, fax: (905) 689-6566
Canadian Explorer Series: rambling roses	Park and Tilford Gardens, North Vancouver	Hortico Nurseries, Ontario, fax: (905) 689-6566
H.M. Eddie and Sons roses	Ornamental Gardens, Summerland	Hortico Nurseries, Ontario, fax: (905) 689-6566
Jalbert mini roses	Select Roses, Langley	Select Roses, Langley (604) 530-5786
Mander mini roses	Centennial Garden, Coquitlam	Fraser Pacific Rose Society, (604) 462-7249
Timothy Eaton hybrid tea	Portland International Rose Test Garden, Oregon	Hortico Nurseries, Ontario, fax: (905) 689-6566

Rural Gardens: Greater Vancouver

Burvilla House

This early 1900s Queen Anne-style residence is filled with collectibles, many of which are for sale. Visitors can picnic on the dyke and watch the river's marine traffic. Garden-lovers will enjoy this heritage home's small gardens, designed to evoke nostalgia for simpler times and the wholesome rural life. Admission is free, and the garden is wheelchair accessible.

Location: Travel south from George Massey Tunnel, follow sign for "Victoria Ferry-River Road," turn east on River Road and follow the signs, Delta.

Haney House

The furniture and household items of this recently restored 1878 pioneer farmhouse and garden represent three generations of the Haney family. In summer, afternoon tea is served occasionally on the verandah next to the flower patch. Phone ahead to arrange tea. These tiny, nostalgic gardens feature rural-style flower beds of mixed perennials and annuals that bloom in late July and August. Admission is free. Wheelchair accessibility in the garden is good; accessibility in the house is fair.

Location: 11612-224th Street, Maple Ridge.

London Heritage Farm

Charles and William London, two brothers who built this home in 1877, were industrious

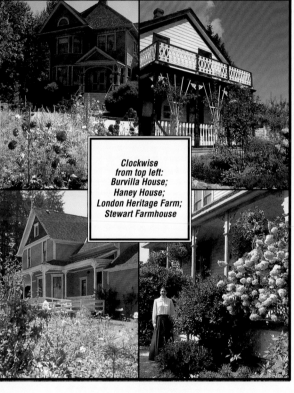

Clockwise from top left:
Burvilla House;
Haney House;
London Heritage Farm;
Stewart Farmhouse

dyke builders who assumed an active role in their community. In 1978, their quaint farmhouse and 2 ha (4.6 acres) of adjoining land were designated a heritage site. The home has been restored in keeping with 1901 standards. A large kitchen garden is planted each year, and there are delightful flower borders and vines around the home's perimeter. Phone for details and summer event list: (604) 271-5220. Admission is free. Wheelchair accessibility to the garden is good; accessibility to the house is fair.

Location: 6511 Dyke Road, Richmond. Turn left on Dyke Road near the south foot of No. 2 Road.

Stewart Farmhouse

The remaining remnants of a dedicated gardener's lifetime work are found here. A few years ago, the fruit trees began to suffer and the perennials struggled to survive. Fortunately, a new Heritage funding program has restored this 1890s farmhouse and its gardens beautiful.

From time to time, weavers practice their craft in the Hooser Weaving Centre.

Admission is free or by donation; guided tours operate on weekends. The garden and house are wheelchair accessible.

Location: Elgin Heritage Park, 13723 Crescent Road, South Surrey.

Left: "And 'tis my faith that every flower enjoys the air it breathes."
—William Wordsworth, 1810

Stanley Park's Gardens: Vancouver

The Rose Garden

Planted in 1920 by the Kiwanis organization, this popular rose garden is a fragrant stopover in June and early July. More popular than Stanley Park's nearby "secret" Shakespearean Garden and arboretum, the rose garden's hundreds of climbers, grandifloras and hybrid teas are grouped by colour. Some of the beds are labeled: Queen Elizabeth, Ingrid Bergman, William Shakespeare, Big Purple, Tiffany, Sunburst, Alexander, and Pristine. The Stanley Park police, mounted on shiny black horses, frequently pass by on their way back to the stables.

Grandiflora is a "manufactured" class—specifically invented for the Queen Elizabeth rose, a cultivar introduced in 1954 by Germain's Nursery in the U.S.A. A cross of Charlotte Armstrong, a hybrid tea, and Floradora, a Floribunda, the Queen Elizabeth represents attempts in the 1950s to produce a different rose. It was hybridized to display the long stems, large blooms and the pointed buds of the hybrid teas, combined with the hardiness and flower clusters of the shrubbier Floribundas. Grandifloras, have a tendency to grow tall and produce large flowers, both singly and in clusters on the stem. Their gangly growth and individual florets are larger than standard Floribundas. The United States and Canada both recognize the Grandiflora as a separate class in rose competitions, while the International

Beyond Stanley Park's Rose Garden in the distance is the Shakespearean Garden and its arboretum of English trees.

rose community (notably Great Britain) continues to lump them in with hybrid teas and refer to them as "large-flowered modern roses."

Admission to Stanley Park's Rose Garden is free; parking requires a compulsory fee. The area is wheelchair accessible.

Location: In Stanley Park at the foot of Georgia Street, Vancouver. The Rose Garden is near the Stanley Park Pavilion; upon entering the Park, take the left fork, straight ahead.

Frederick Law Olmsted

A visitor from New York once noted the similarity between Stanley Park and Central Park. It was an astute observation. Much of this park's design is based on the principles of Frederick Law Olmsted (1822-1903), the masterful designer of New York's Central Park, Brooklyn's Prospect Park, Washington DC's Capitol Grounds, Boston's park system, Chicago's World's Fair, California's Yosemite National Park and Montreal's Parc Royale. Having developed his design principles during a landscaping tour of England in 1850, this American owes much to the English Picturesque tradition. He often said that he wished to eliminate the tradition of formal or geometric gardening, and to find a true, natural style. His role in designing in Stanley Park has resulted in a truly wonderful park.

Grandiflora, "Queen Elizabeth"

Ted and Mary Greig Rhododendron Garden: Stanley Park

Hidden away in a corner of Stanley Park, the Ted and Mary Greig Rhododendron Garden is a gem. A meandering walkway curves through azaleas, rhododendrons,

Due to the moderating moisture-laden breezes from the nearby ocean the Greig Garden has its own micro-climate. It blooms up to a week earlier than Vancouver's other show gardens.

camellias, magnolias, maple and cherry trees. The area is radiant in April and May. Magnolia trees burst into flower first, then camellias and tulips,

the handkerchief or dove tree, rhododendrons, and finally, by azaleas and late-blooming rhododendrons.

Retired Stanley Park head gardener Allayne Cook believes this part of the park is truly wonderful. "Though it was primarily designed for the enjoyment of people in the nearby high rise buildings, sailors from visiting ships seem especially drawn to this part of the park." Cook has long been devoted to the gardens. "I worked for the Parks Board for almost 40 years," he says. "They told me my first job was to move 8,000 rhododendrons to this part of the park, and I just took it from there."

The area owes its name to the Greigs, who donated their extensive and mature rhododendron collection to the Park many decades ago. It has benefited from the special attention of being next to Vancouver's Parks Board office and chambers, and is thus subject to the periodic scrutiny of elected municipal councilors.

Information on park wildlife, vegetation and guided nature walks is available from Stanley Park's Nature House on Lost Lagoon, (604) 257-8544. Admission to the gardens is free. There is a compulsory parking fee. The area is wheelchair accessible.

Location: For access to the Greig Rhododendron Garden, travel around the park to Second Beach and park by the Parks Board Office or at the Tea House.

Magnolia Trees in Stanley Park

Commonly associated with the deep south and mint juleps, the one southern magnolia tree in the Greig Rhododendron Garden does quite poorly. Of greater interest are the 20 varieties of hardy northerns that burst into bloom in early April. Magnolias take from 10 to 17 springtimes to muster the energy to flower in full. They devote their first spring burst entirely to their flowering cycle, which occurs before they put out a single leaf. A mature example of one variety, the M. Barbara Cook, was carefully hybridized in Vancouver by Stanley Park's former head gardener, Mr. Allayne Cook. It is due to be released in

Early magnolia

several local nurseries. Admission is free, and the area is wheelchair accessible.
Location: The magnolia trees are in the Ted and Mary Greig Rhododendron Garden at Stanley Park.

Special Interest Commercial Gardens

On the eastern outskirts of Vancouver in Langley and Maple Ridge, there are a number of commercial facilities. Not only do these nurseries and farms have free public show gardens, they also hold periodic fairs, art displays and festivals for the enjoyment of avid gardeners.

For example, Warrington Farms has a fall festival complete with apple cider, pumpkins and dried flower arranging demonstrations. Others, such as Erikson's Daylilies, are the official Canadian producers or distributors for their lines. Many now have Web pages on the internet. Please call ahead before making a visit to any of the facilities listed. Many are closed when their displays are out of season.

Rainforest Gardens, boasts a thriving commercial nursery noted for its propagation of unusually hardy specimens, as well as a lovely acreage and public gardens. Ken and Elke Knechtel conduct periodic walking tours of the nursery and its gardens, inviting guest speakers to discuss various topics from "container gardening" to the biology of gardens. Their greatest pride is the White Garden which is at its best in July and August. Call for a current program or drop in to see the show garden. Tour information is available from (604) 467-4218. A catalogue is available. Admission is free and the area is wheelchair accessible.

Location: 13139 224th Street, Maple Ridge.

Commercial Nurseries with Show Gardens

A free list of Garden Centres in your area is available from the B.C. Nursery Trades Association/Landscape B.C., (604) 574-7772, fax (604) 574-7773. The listings below differ from ordinary city nurseries because they feature large display gardens, open fields and country settings.

Brookside Orchid Garden	Orchid selections	23779-32nd Avenue, Langley (604) 533-8286
Erikson's Daylily Gardens	Award-winning daylilies	24642-51st Avenue, Langley (604) 856-5758
Ferncliff Gardens	Award-winning dahlias	8394 McTaggert Street, Mission (604) 826-2447
Foxglove Everlasting Flower Farm	Dried flowers, cottage, display garden	6741-224th street, Langley (604) 888-4141
Gray's Flower Farm	Flower fields	20104 - 8th Avenue, Langley (604) 534-5161
Lilyponds Canada	Water lilies and Water irises	11202 Stave Lake Road, Mission (604) 820-864
Meadowsweet Farms Garden Nursery	Retail cottage nursery, fields	24640-16th Avenue, Langley (604) 530-2611
Rain Forest Nurseries	Country setting	1470-227th Street, Langley (604) 530-3499
Rainforest Gardens	Hardy perennials and alpines	13139-224th Street, Maple Ridge (604) 467-4218
Select Roses, Brad Jalbert	Rose gardens	22771-38th Avenue, Langley (604) 530-5786
Landscape Depot	Water displays	19779-56th Avenue, Langley (604) 533-7371
Warrington Flower Farms	Gardens, dried materials, Little Red Barn store	240th Street between Lougheed Highway and Dewdney Trunk Road, Maple Ridge (604) 467-7555

Special Interest Gardens: Surrey

Bear Creek Garden

First cleared in 1973, this 2 ha (5 acre) municipal flower garden is located in the midst of a busy community. It developed gradually, eventually amassing a collection of rhododendrons, azaleas, heathers, heaths and ornamental grasses. Showy seasonal bedding displays add mounds of colour in summer. Surrounded by a forest of second growth cedar, cottonwood and alder, King Creek is a pleasant feature located on the edge of the gardens. It runs with salmon in November and December. The paved path system provides easy walking. Admission is free, and the area is wheelchair accessible.

Location: 13750-88th Avenue, Surrey.

City Hall Gardens: Surrey

The bedding plants, totem pole, picnic spots, bubbling waterfalls and surrounding forest make this one of the most impressive garden acreages surrounding any municipal hall. Bridal parties wander in and out on summer Saturdays, and the on-site coffee shop makes for a refreshing conclusion to a stroll in the garden.

The garden is always open and admission is free. The area is mostly wheelchair accessible.

Location: 14245-56th Avenue, Surrey.

Dartshill Garden

The Francisca Darts Garden or "Dartshill Garden," as it is coming

Clockwise from top left: Bear Creek; City Hall, Surrey; Dartshill; Peace Arch

to be known, is a 2.8 ha (7 acre) garden with a plant collection that rivals that of many botanical gardens. Presently a private garden, it is deeded to the municipality. It was featured in the television series "Northwest Gardens" as one of the primary gardens defining Northwest Garden style.

Dartshill is occasionally open for garden society tours.

Surrey Parks and Recreation: (604) 501-5050. Wheelchair accessibility is fair.

Location: Ask for directions when booking.

Peace Arch Gardens

Canada and the United States celebrate their long friendship with two gardens that bump up against each other at the Douglas International Crossing. A tall, white memorial with open gates bears the inscription, "May these gates never close." Each year in early June, flower lovers from the two nations stop to smell the roses and hold a "Hands Across the Border" parade to celebrate that friendship. Phone (604) 531-3068. Admission is free, and the area is partly wheelchair accessible.

Location: 138 Peace Arch Park Drive, on the border between Surrey B.C., and Blaine, WA.

Asian Garden

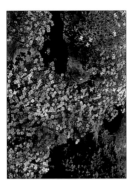

Alpine Garden

Native Plant Garden

Food Garden

Physick Garden

U.B.C Botanical Garden

Established with specimens cultivated on the Riverview Lands by "Botany John" Davidson before 1916, the University of British Columbia's Botanical Garden is one of the oldest university gardens in Canada; see pages 95 and 120. Located high on a cliff overlooking the Pacific Ocean's Strait of Georgia, over 10,000 different varieties of

trees, shrubs and flowers grow under the watchful eye of university researchers. Ongoing studies are conducted on a wide variety of flora from the world's temperate zones, and U.B.C. now sponsors a program to introduce native plants to the gardening public. While the facility's overall layout is pleasant enough, the 28 ha (70 acre) site is primarily a research garden. Many landscape designers believe that garden trends are moving

away from consciously designed artifices toward a wilder, natural look. The popularity of this specimen and research garden testifies to this projection.

The David C. Lam Asian Garden is located in the midst of a mature British Columbia forest of grand fir, Douglas fir, western hemlock, and western red cedar. Some of the 400-year-old trees provide a convenient resting place for bald eagles. The main path, called the Asian Way, has several sub-paths named after early plant explorers. Like Victorian plant hunters who travelled to Asiatic regions to collect exotic plants, modern plant hunters have assembled a wide variety of Asian species here: woody groundcovers, low-lying shrubs and flowers such as rhododendrons, maples, viburnums, clematis, roses and shade-loving perennials. The botanical richness of Asia continues to astound us.

The E.H. Lohbrunner Alpine Garden, a long, narrow alpine garden of rock-clinging specimens is located on a sunny west-facing slope. Named after an early British Columbia resident who loved rock gardens, it allows visitors to experience the low-lying

U.B.C. Botanical Garden	
Admission charged	Yes. Discount in effect, if combining with admission to Nitobe Memorial Garden.
Wheelchair access	Mostly accessible
Telephone	Garden Shop, (604) 822-4208; Garden Pavilion Rental, (604) 822-4804
Location	University of British Columbia Campus, 6804 S.W. Marine Drive, 16th Avenue and S.W. Marine Drive, Vancouver

Left: "To have complete satisfaction from flowers you must have time to spend with them. There must be rapport. I talk to them and they talk to me."—Princess Grace of Monaco

vegetation of the Himalayas, the Alps, the Rockies, the Andes and other mountainous regions of the world. Probably one the most nostalgic mountain blooms are the lovely spring stands of Edelweiss from the Austrian Alps.

Within the **B.C. Native Garden** are habitat niches ranging from lowland to rainforest providing a fertile environment for indigenous plants. A sinuous stone path meanders through the bog and crosses a rustic bridge. The area is surrounded by free-growing tussocks of sphagnum moss, Labrador tea, bog laurel, cranberries and sundews. Wild strawberries peek through the forest floor.

Skunk cabbages grow here, too. These yellow flowers are surprisingly popular in Europe, where they act as harbingers of spring and even appear in commercial floral arrangements.

The newly restored **Physick Garden** is formally laid out to reflect the growing interest in medicinal applications for plants. Centered by a bronze sundial, this 16th century-style garden introduces the public to humble plants continuing to prove therapeutic (or at least beneficial) to humans. Many of these herbals and botanicals originate from England's Chelsea Physic Garden; see page 38.

The **Food Garden** is surrounded by berries and a collection of orchard trees trained to stay low for easy harvesting. Fruit tree techniques include cordons—oblique, single, double, triple and multiple—and espaliers—fan, palmette, horizontal,

candelabra and Belgian fence.

The **Winter Garden** is designed to show colour from fall until early spring. Masses of heathers, fragrant Viburnums, early Witch Hazels and early bulbs all put on their best during Vancouver's rainy gloom. There are also good examples of berried holly bushes.

From late spring to late fall, the perennial borders are a visual delight. Ornamental grasses blend in with rare perennials from around the world. The Asian-looking **Garden Pavilion** located here is available for conferences, seminars, weddings, banquets, receptions and barbecues. Admission is charged; discounts are in effect if you combine your visit with a trip to Nitobe Memorial Garden. The area is mostly wheelchair accessible. Phone (604) 822-4208 (Garden shop) or (604) 822-4804 (Garden Pavilion Rental). The horticultural line answers garden questions, (604) 822-5858. Plant sales, lunchtime mini lectures and non-credit courses are held.

Location: University of British Columbia Campus, 6804 S.W. Marine Drive, 16th Avenue and S.W. Marine Drive, Vancouver.

Garden Events in Greater Vancouver

Vancouver's garden clubs are active and there are thousands of avid gardeners in the area. Dozens of organizations put on hundreds of shows and plant sales each year. To find out about upcoming shows and events, contact one of the following organizations or newspapers.

• VanDusen Botanical Garden acts a clearinghouse for many garden clubs (604) 878-9274
• Vancouver Sun newspaper listings on Saturdays
• Consult the Internet Keyword: Hedgerows
• Vancouver Tourism InfoCentre (604) 683-2000

What Is a Botanical Garden?

In contrast to show gardens, display gardens and parks, botanical gardens are meant to be living museums. Their plants are collections—scientifically organized—designed to display and more importantly, to preserve certain species. At various times, botanical gardens are used for taxonomic studies, herbarium exchanges, rare plants research, selection and breeding experiments and student projects. Additionally, botanical gardens fulfill their mandate by educating the public, increasing general appreciation for plant life and introducing new plants to the market.

Himalayan blue poppy

The Saga of the Golden Spruce

"LEGENDARY TREE'S LOSS SICKENS RESIDENTS," proclaimed front page headlines one January day in 1997. A 300-year-old Sitka spruce tree, valued for its unusual golden needles, had been maliciously chopped down. Of considerable importance to the Haida people, the mature tree stood more than 50 m (150 feet) high with a diametre of 196 cm (6.4 feet). It was felled by a transient who left scattered notes expressing his rage toward university-trained professionals "responsible for all the abominations of life on this planet." Alone in the rainy forest, he took two days to chop the giant tree down.

The magnificent mutation stood near tiny Sandburg, in the remote forests of the Queen Charlotte Islands, off B.C.'s west coast. Its golden colour was caused by a chlorophyll deficiency, making it a rarity, and it was said that all attempts to reproduce it met with failure—shoots and seeds would never grow. In summer, the golden tree attracted a steady stream of visitors who learned of it mostly by word of mouth.

For the Haida people, the unique tree was revered. According to their stories, the tree was once a boy named K'iid K'iyaas who, along with his grandfather, was the only survivor of a terrible snowstorm. As they dug themselves out, grandfather warned him not to look back. But he could not resist and as he peeked, his feet took

Rare golden spruce

root and he became the tree. Upon word of the tree's destruction, native people, Queen Charlotte residents, and each of the respectful thousands who had made the pilgrimage to see the golden giant were distressed.

The following week, headlines of a different sort began to appear. "RARE GOLDEN SPRUCE TREE SECRETLY REPRODUCED AT U.B.C.," read the headlines. Fearing that if the news leaked out, people would descend upon the islands to obtain their own spruce clippings, Bruce MacDonald, Director of U.B.C. Botanical Gardens, explained that a few experts had successfully carried out limited propagations. They kept mum about their work. He identified two fledging offspring of the Queen Charlotte "mother," which had been growing without fanfare for many years in a public area of U.B.C.'s research garden. The trees were given to the garden in 1978 by the late Gordon Bentham, a collector of rare

conifers. Indeed, the rare golden clippings were considered a prize. Forest magnate H.R. MacMillan had secretly grown one in his private garden, but it withered away at the age of 15. Pat Carney, a former Canadian cabinet minister, cautiously admitted that she too had secretly owned one. For various reasons, their offspring all expired. Scientists descended on the fallen tree to take more clippings before it withered away. To date, however, no shoot has ever survived beyond 30 years; the parent plant was 300 years old.

As the saga continued, the New York Times and newspapers around the world picked up the story. The vagrant was charged with mischief and as the investigation proceeded, he seemed to have rather strong links to a native band who are traditional enemies of the Haida. The plot thickened.

Back on the Queen Charlottes, the Haida Nation followed the news with mixed emotions. On the one hand, they were displeased to discover so many shoots had been secretly taken; on the other, they graciously accepted a gift, from the university, of the best of two shoots they had grown for the past 18 years. The remaining little mutant tree, grown from the Queen Charlotte Mother, is available for public viewing at U.B.C. Botanical Garden. Its rare golden needles are pictured here. See it for yourself.

VanDusen is not only a major showgarden, it is the information clearinghouse for many garden-related workshops, lectures, seminars, events, shows, plant sales and heritage seed exchanges in Greater Vancouver.

VanDusen Botanical Garden: Vancouver

In 1910, this site was an isolated bush-covered acreage owned by the Canadian Pacific Railway (CPR). The Shaughnessy Golf Club took over the property and leased it until 1960, when it made a decision to move. However, the subsequent plan to turn the golf course into a housing development met with stiff local opposition. In 1966, the land was purchased with funding from the City of Vancouver, the Government of British Columbia and the

The Heron Fountain

Vancouver Botanical Gardens Association, aided by a generous donation from Mr. W.J. VanDusen. A full botanical garden officially opened on August 30, 1975. Today, this major display garden is administered by the Vancouver Parks Department, the VanDusen Botanical Gardens Association and the help of over 400 volunteers. Together they make this Vancouver facility the central focus for gardeners' educational programs, garden events, shows and competitions, and the Master Gardening Certificate Program.

Some say that the landscaping style of the B.C. coast is still evolving. VanDusen Gardens reflects this concept. Its sub-gardens or "garden rooms" have an imported character, each a composite of romantic or functional images from other places. Landscape development at these gardens was carried out under the direction of Bill Livingstone from 1971 to 1976 and under Curator R. Roy Forster from 1977 to 1996,. The Floral Hall and Garden Pavilion were designed by the firm Underwood, McKinley, Wilson and Smith with Herb Wilson as designer and architect. The award-winning Forest Centre was designed by Thompson, Berwick, Pratt and Partners with Paul Merrick as design architect.

Allow ample time to visit this 22 ha (55 acre) garden, its 7,500 plants, two totem poles, two lakes, two ponds and various buildings. A weeping blue atlas cedar stands at the entrance to the little White Garden, gleaming in milky floral splendor. The traditional Herb Garden displaying culinary herbs and other savory favourites is followed by the Stanley Smith Rock Garden, a little rockery with year-round dwarf conifers and a weeping sequoia. The pool and its miniature water lilies are bordered by beds of ever-changing bulbs. The formal Rose Garden, in a geometric Renaissance style, is planted with hybrid tea, floribunda and shrub roses around a central sundial.

Deep in the garden, the Laburnum Walk is nestled in a stand of oak trees and tree roses. Tree roses are created by

Left: Livingstone Lake "Keep your face to the sunshine and you cannot see the shadow." Helen Keller

"It is at the edge of a petal that love waits." —William Carlos Williams, American poet (1883-1963)

grafting normal roses onto tall, stalky rose plants. The Lathhouse provides the frame for summer's lush hanging baskets. Through an archway of weeping beeches is the Perennial Garden. The island style of bordering displays hardy perennials and features dramatic ornamental grasses. The nearby Heather Garden, especially lilting in late winter, is accessible by crossing a little stone bridge. Past the white birches are the stone grotto, Livingstone Lake, Cypress Pond, and Heron Lake. These massive landscaping additions allow the VanDusen facility to exhibit fully mature species in their finest settings. Throughout the garden are more than 110 species of pine, most native to the northern hemisphere. The two lakes are home to many water lilies and for those who miss their home "Down Under," the Southern Hemisphere Collection is located across from the lakes. An extensive area of the garden is devoted to Asian vegetation, but for aficionados, the Elizabethan hedge maze, formed from over a thousand pruned Pyramid cedars, is the must-

see. Art lovers will also find 20 assorted sculptures and fountains throughout the gardens.

Spring bursts in with an impressive display of magnolia flowers, some a foot in diameter; late spring is glorious with symphonies of rhododendrons along Rhododendron Walk, and after the glories of summer fade, brightly coloured leaves tint the landscape in the Autumn Colour Arboretum. Prolific highlights include the fern dell, a quiet area of assorted ferns and the new Canadian Heritage Garden. The Fragrance Garden features ro-

tating seasonal displays in raised concrete planters. And finally, VanDusen is home to brightberried hollies; an entire area is devoted to 147 varieties of the prickly Christmas bush.

Special events in the Floral Hall include heritage seed exchanges, ikebana workshops, a mediaeval fair with people in costume on the Great Lawn, and an annual compost sale. Garden club shows and demonstrations occur almost every week in summer.

Afternoon Tea in Vancouver

While nearby Victoria is reveling in its English Breakfast, coffee is Vancouver's speciality. However, the tea bastion remains solid in the following establishments.

'T' Oasis in Nobo Tea Room	881 Herrmann Street, Coquitlam (604) 874-8320
Burnaby Heritage Village, (The Royal Treatment)	6501 Deer Lake Ave, Burnaby (604) 293-6525
Sprinkler's Restaurant at VanDusen Botanical Garden	5251 Oak Street at 37th Avenue, Vancouver (604) 261-0011
Sutton Place Hotel	845 Burrard Street, Vancouver (604) 682-5511
Tearoom T	2460 Heather Street, Vancouver (604) 874-8320
The Bacchus Lounge, Wedgewood Hotel	845 Hornby Street, Vancouver (604) 689-7777

Information: VanDusen Botanical Garden

Type	Premier municipal display garden, garden show host, educational
Size	22 ha (55 acres)
Time allotment	2 to 4 hours
Open	10 a.m. to variable closing hours; if concerned, phone ahead.
Year round	Yes
Best seasons	Late spring, summer, autumn
Sub-gardens	Children's Garden, White Garden, Herb Garden, Rock Garden, Food Garden, bulbs, Rose Garden, Lathhouse, bonsai, Perennial Garden, Heather Garden, stone grotto, lakes, floating bridge, Southern Hemisphere Collection, Fragrance Garden, Autumn Colour Arboretum, Rhododendron Walk, fern dell, hydrangeas, Canadian Heritage Garden, Holly Garden, Asian plant section, Maze Garden
Additional features	Sprinkler's Restaurant, Floral Hall, library, classrooms
Events	There are many special events; phone for information. Festival of Lights (December) ; Annual VanDusen plant sale (late April); All British Field Meet of classic cars (mid-May); VanDusen Flower and Garden Show (early June); Master Gardeners Program; numerous flower club shows, workshops, lectures, classes, demonstrations
Admission charged	Yes; however, 1 or 2 winter days each year are free (as a public service); phone ahead.
Wheelchair access	Good, mostly accessible. Allow time to rest.
Guided tours	By arrangement, and every Sunday at 2 p.m. Maps are available at the entrance.
Telephone	(604) 878-9274
Additional services	Sprinkler's Restaurant, (604) 261-0011; Master gardeners will answer home gardening questions, (604) 257-8662; guide-driven electric carts are available for those with limited walking ability (Easter to Thanksgiving).
Location	5251 Oak Street at 37th Avenue, Vancouver
Nearby attractions	U.B.C. Botanical Garden, Nitobe Memorial Garden, Bloedel Conservatory in Queen Elizabeth Park

VanDusen's Sino-Himalayan Garden

Many common garden plants we take for granted today originate from Asiatic nations. Three compelling reasons British Columbia takes particular note of Asia's botanical resources are Vancouver's geographic position on the Pacific Rim, its large Asian population, and the debt of gratitude all gardeners owe to Asia.

When Queen Victoria came to the throne in 1839, China was closed to all but a few French Jesuit missionaries. With difficulty, these modest men smuggled a few seeds out of its forbidden territories. These

Korean Pavilion

tantalizing morsels whetted the appetites of various horticultural interests, particularly Kew Botanic Gardens in England. As soon as the Opium Wars ended in 1842 and for a century thereafter, British and American interests supported plant-gathering expeditions to the Himalayan regions. These were followed by

breeding and hybridizing programs in France and England. Many of the plant and flowers now considered garden staples had their origins in Asia's mountain valleys and plains. E.H. Wilson is the name most commonly associated with these expeditions. A few examples of his acquisitions are: rhododendrons, lilies, magnolias, camellias, primulas, wisteria, many rose crosses and many familiar trees. This large section of VanDusen Garden reminds us how much all gardeners owe these explorers.

113

Wedding Gardens in Vancouver

On any Saturday afternoon in summer at Queen Elizabeth Park, wedding parties arrive and leave with the regularity of airplanes at a busy airport. There are brides on the pathways, in the flowerbeds, on the lawns, along the bridge, inside the sculptures, beside the waterfall, down in the quarry, and even perched on the cliffs. There are lost and bewildered wedding guests and bridesmaids with nothing to do. There are shy flower girls, and best men who are in a playful mood. There are even brides who misplace their own wedding parties! As one onlooker to this silk chiffon scene said, " If a man isn't careful, he could go home with the wrong bride!"

Anyone casually visiting the garden may discreetly enjoy the festivities. These photographs were taken during prime bridal party viewing time in Queen Elizabeth Park, any summer Saturday from 1 p.m. to 4 p.m. Drop in and experience the bridal landings for yourself.

Wedding Gardens in Greater Vancouver

These gardens have indicated that they welcome bridal parties and garden wedding photo shoots with advance notice. The public is welcome to watch the proceedings.

Centennial Rose Garden	Coquitlam
Centennial Gardens	Burnaby
Fantasy Garden World	Richmond
Friendship Gardens	New Westminster
Hart House on Deer Lake	Burnaby
Memorial Park Gardens	West Vancouver
Minoru Chapel and Pierrefond Gardens	Richmond
Minter Gardens	Rosedale (Bridal Falls)
Nitobe Memorial Garden	Vancouver
Park and Tilford Gardens	North Vancouver
Peace Arch Gardens	White Rock
Queen Elizabeth Park	Vancouver
Sendall Gardens	Langley
Stanley Park (Gardens)	Vancouver
VanDusen Botanical Garden	Vancouver
Whytecliff Park	West Vancouver

Water Garden Koi Fish

As evidenced in symbols, in ancient paintings, pottery, ornaments and carvings, the wild brown carp has long been a sign of success in Asian countries. During the 1800s, primarily in Japan, the science of controlled breeding was used to develop special carps for garden ponds. Naturally coloured brown carps were carefully interbred to produce red and white mutations called Hi-Goi, now known inside Japan as Nishikigoi, and later shortened outside Japan to Koi. In 1915, a tricoloured Koi was first introduced to the public during an exhibit in Tokyo. Breeding methods were closely guarded and a Koi was extremely expensive.

In 1920, in Germany, a shiny offspring bred from a wild mirror carp resulted in gold or silver scales, now considered essential by some owners. It is argued that the finest Koi are still found in Japan, Hong Kong or China, but the growing popularity of the hobby around the world has reduced the price of individual fish to more affordable levels. Today, regular varieties sell for $10 to $200 each, though prize breeding specimens can surpass $20,000. A high-quality, non-breeding fish, suitable for an indoor pond, in the waiting lounge of an upscale Chinese restaurant or the offices of a Singapore brokerage firm, might cost about $1000.

Koi are showy garden pond fish, bred to exhibit their brightest markings when viewed from the top. At full maturity, they grow to approximately 1 m (2 to 3 feet) and weigh in at about 15 kg (35 pounds.) Because of their size, they are normally kept in large ponds with at least 1,500 gallons of well-filtered water. They can tolerate some winter cold.

Koi Clubs are active throughout the world and with the newly evolving craze of water gardening, Koi Festivals, events, auctions and displays are starting in many communities. Koi clubs are an exciting way to learn the details of this fascinating hobby and there are many listings on the internet.

After many years of breeding expertise, the Japanese now recognize several complex lineages and these are generally accepted throughout the world. Based on a Koi's markings, colours and scale types, one can determine the subcategory to which an individual fish belongs. With so many Koi being bred for garden ponds throughout the world, it is not unusual to find totally unique combinations.

Koi Fish Classifications

Buying a Koi fish is a bit like buying a basic car and adding options or features to upgrade it. When the following words are applied to the classification, they refer to an acceptable modification of the basic class. • Doitsu: scaleless version • Gin-Rin: metallic version • Tancho: additional round red spot on head • Bekko: additional black markings.

Koi Fish Viewing in Greater Vancouver

Listed here are public facilities where Koi are part of the display. In addition, there are many commercial facilities that now sell Koi fish. An annual Koi Festival is held at Lilyponds Canada in Mission; see page 123.

Bloedel Floral Conservatory	Vancouver
Dr. Sun Yat-Sen Classical Chinese Garden	Vancouver
Nitobe Memorial Garden	Vancouver
Unique Koi and Water Gardens (retail outlet)	11761-272nd St., Maple Ridge

Tiptoe through the tulips at the Bradner Bulb Gardens.

Fraser Valley Gardens

Bradner Bulb Gardens: Abbotsford

For centuries, the Netherlands have dominated bulb commerce. At present, its horticultural sector produces approximately nine billion flower bulbs: seven billion for export; two billion for domestic use. Evenly distributed, this makes for almost two flower bulbs for every person on the planet. If placed four inches apart, it is said that the yearly bulb production of the Netherlands would circle the equator seven times. The most popular exports are tulips (three billion), followed by lilies, gladioli, daffodils and hyacinths. The United States leads the bulb import market, followed by Germany and Japan. Over the years, western Canada has attracted a number of Holland's immigrants—experts in floriculture. Many settled in the Fraser Valley. A delightful way to herald spring is to visit the commercial bulb display fields founded by several of these enterprising experts, located within an hour's drive of Vancouver. In mid-April, bobbing fields of daffodils with names like Fortissimo, Rosy Sunrise, and Mount Hood do indeed "dance in the breeze." In

Bradner Flower Show: Abbotsford

Since 1928, the Bradner Flower Show has been staged in a little community hall. For April timing information and directions to the show hall, contact the Abbotsford Visitor Centre (604) 859-9651. A small admission is charged; the area is wheelchair accessible. Location: on Bradner Road, near Townshipline Road, west of Abbotsford.

Left: "For lo, the winter is past, the rain is over and gone; The flowers appear on the earth." —Song of Solomon

Tulip Frenzies

The first tulips known to Europeans arrived in 1545 via an Austrian Envoy in Turkey, Mr. Ogier Ghiselin de Busbecq. He shipped certain "tulband" bulbs to the Imperial Medicinal Gardens in Vienna. From there, Clusius, a Viennese court gardener and later a professor in Holland, popularized them. For years, bulbs circulated uneventfully; discards ended up in cottager's plots.

Said to resemble the Turkish tulband (turban), the flower's name was corrupted to "tulipan" and later "tulip." However, in 1634, Holland's middle classes, ever anxious to enter the world of big business, discovered that the upper classes were willing to pay handsomely for bulbs producing mutated blooms. Sensing a get-rich-quick scheme, ordinary people began to barter in bulbs. Within months, Tulip Futures soared, and rare bulbs escalated to the price of a farm. Tulip traders

earned up to 60,000 florins (today approximately $44,000) a month—not a bad commission even by modern standards. Fortunes were amassed overnight. In Paris, chique fashions featured raw tulip bulbs thrust into a lady's neckline. As the wave crested, an otherwise sensible brewer swapped his entire brewery for one bulb. In April 1637, the Dutch government

decreed that all Tulip Futures be honoured. Within two months, power brokers and investors alike were in ruin.

Tulips have strange powers. In about 1720 in Turkey, Sultan Ahmed III became obsessed with the chalice-shaped flower. Istanbul's palaces were soon festooned with tulip decorations; high taxes were placed on bulb trading; textiles bore tulip designs. To curry favour with the Sultan, nobles spent fortunes on gifts of rare tulip bulbs; tulip poems were written; a Tulip Guild was formed. By 1730, the Tulip Era or Lala Devre caused the Sultan's downfall. Today Turkey, the homeland of this captivating flower, continues to hold many grand tulip festivals.

Meaningful Flower for Canadians: the Tulip

In 1942, with war raging in Europe, the Crown Princess Juliana of the Netherlands and her family fled their homeland. In 1943, Juliana's baby—a little princess—was born in Ottawa. To make the plight of the displaced royals a little less painful, the Canadian government decreed the hospital birth-room as Dutch soil; a solitary foreign flag flew from Ottawa's Peace Tower; and its carillon bells played Holland's national anthem. The baby girl's chosen name, Margriet—"daisy" was said to represent not only

innocence, but freedom. Two years later, Canadian Allied Forces liberated the Netherlands.

When the family returned home, Princess Juliana and the Dutch people sent Canada a thank-you gift—100,000 tulip

bulbs. Thousands of new bulbs continue to arrive each year. Today, about three million tulips bloom in Canada's capital region and a week-long Canadian Tulip Festival takes place in mid-May.

Throughout the rest of Canada, too, tulips have acquired a special meaning. They represent both the valour of Canadian soldiers and the importance of international friendship.

addition to the familiar golden yellow Alfreds, other varieties display hoops, flounces and elongated centre

cups in a range of whites, salmons and pinks.

As the daffodils fade, tulips come into their glory. Acres of tulips stretch to the horizon. With imaginative names like Orange Emperor, Apricot Beauty, Monte Carlo, Merry Widow and Angelique, they come in a variety of chalice shapes, colour variegations and shredded "parrot" petals.

West Coast Spring Bulbs in Order of Blossoming

Name	Month of appearance	Length of bloom
Snowdrops	January or February	1 to 2 weeks
Anemones/crocus	mid- to late February	2 to 4 weeks
Daffodils	March or April	1 to 5 weeks
Hyacinths	late March or April	2 to 5 weeks
Tulips	mid- to late April	2 to 6 weeks
Ranunucula	April or May	2 to 3 months

At present, the ultimate goal of the tulip world is to produce a perfect black tulip. So far, there are several very deep purples, but true black did not exist until March 1997, when Dutch breeders announced a "black" tulip was ready for market. To see both daffodils and tulip fields in bloom in the Fraser Valley, plan on two separate visits three weeks apart. Phone for details, (604) 856-4923. Admission is free. This is a commercial facility; a catalogue is available. Wheelchair accessibility is adequate; no public washrooms.

Location: 6735 Bradner Road, near Abbotsford.

Friendship Garden: Hope

In 1942, during the dark days of World War II, a jittery Canadian nation forcibly removed 20,000 Japanese immigrants and many who were long-time Canadian citizens from their homes, seized their possessions, sold their property and placed them

Members of the Japanese community help the municipality maintain their garden.

in stark internment camps. One such camp, Tashme, was located east of Hope.

Though most internees recall this as a severe, depressing time, it is a testimony to the strength of the human spirit that one old gentleman at Roseberry Camp, near Ladner, set out to create a Japanese garden. Growing what shrubbery and vegetables he

could scrounge, he made garden ornaments out of peeled pine. Every day he worked hard, neatly raking tiny gravel paths among his meagre plantings. Whenever outsiders came to visit the camp's supervisors, the old gardener would disappear and come out in his best clothes: a white shirt, white pants, a dark sash and polished black shoes.

He was very proud to show off his marvelous garden. Sadly, while outsiders tenderly remember his garden, the old man's name has been lost over time.

(Story first told by Barry Broadfoot in *Years of Sorrow, Years of Shame.*)

Out of darkness comes the light. In 1991, several Japanese-Canadians, many once interned near Hope, built a Japanese garden as a gesture of healing and hope for a peaceful future. Admission is free. The area is wheelchair accessible.

Location: In Memorial Park, corner of 3rd Avenue and Wallace Street, Hope.

Floriculture Visits: Fraser Valley

Floriculture, the greenhouse production of flowers, is one of British Columbia's fastest growing agricultural sectors. Since 1986, annual floriculture sales have increased from $46 million to more than $75 million. Over the same period, British Columbia's floriculture greenhouse growing area has increased from 600,000 square metres to almost a million square metres. Over 80 per cent of British Columbia's hothouse or greenhouse flower growers are located in the Lower Mainland and South Coast Region. The B.C. interior has ten per cent of the total floriculture greenhouse area, while Vancouver Island and the Coast have nine per cent.

British Columbia's floriculture industry was established in two phases. During the 1930s, Asian growers developed an ornamental flower industry and after 1945, an influx of European growers, mainly from Holland, specialized in cut flower production, bulb production, and brought

In addition to huge glass hothouses, many Fraser Valley operations produce garden bedding plants for both domestic and export markets.

automation to the industry. Today, it is possible to train in a horticultural program and have a career in daffodil and bulb harvesting, flower packing, greenhouse maintenance, or orchid and rose assistance.

Large public gardens, such as the ones covered in this book, usually have their own greenhouse operations and grow their own annuals. Plant hothouses service two distinct markets: "Dry sales"—bedding plants, seeds and bulbs for

home gardeners and landscapers, and the larger "forced segment"—flowers destined to be sold out of season as cut flowers (bouquets) or pot plants. Supermarkets and florists bid on large quantities of these "forced" blooms at a special auction several times a week. In addition, there are vast B.C. greenhouse operations in hothouse vegetables: tomatoes, cucumbers, peppers and lettuce.

A Rose Growing Operation

Under 0.8 ha (2 acres) of glass, the Lower Mainland's largest florist-rose-growing operation annually produces more than 55,000 rosebuds. Maturing in a crushed coconut shell medium, rosebuds are harvested, racked, trimmed with shears, automatically tied together, stored in a cooler to "harden," and sold at auction. The Van Den Bosch family has been in the florist-rose-growing business since 1948 and Peter Van Den Bosch, Vice

President, says his best sellers are Eskimo, a white rose, and Velvet, a red one (shown here). Though good-natured and open to visitors who call ahead, Peter absolutely refuses to say whether he gives his wife roses for her birthday! Free admission with prior arrangements; (604) 795-3555, fax (604) 793-0355. The area is wheelchair accessible.

Location: Van Den Bosch Greenhouses, 48300 Yale Road East, Chilliwack.

Peter Van Den Bosch

Rural Gardens: Fraser Valley

Agassiz Arboretum

Established in 1888 as the Dominion Experimental Farm, this 665 ha (1,620 acre) research facility has devoted one section to a mature heirloom arboretum. Some of the labeled specimens include a giant sequoia, a Nordman fir, an English oak, a linden tree, a cut-leaf European beech and a ponderosa pine (shown). Nearby are modern facilities for poultry, dairy and greenhouse vegetable research. Also on site is the small Railway Station Museum. Admission is free, and the area is wheelchair accessible.

Agassiz Arboretum

Location: Enter just past the intersection of Highway 7 and Highway 9, Agassiz. The sign reads "Agricultural Research Station."

Clayburn Village Gardens

Starting in 1905, a picturesque village grew up around a industrial brick-making kiln near Sumas Mountain. Workers including the mill foreman and the accountant once utilized the factory's products to build their family homes. The store, school and church followed suit. Later abandoned, the tiny brick community is now privately owned. Present-day residents are making delightful additions, including little white picket fences and quaint cottage gardens. In late July, much of the brick village opens its homes and gardens to the public. Tea and cakes are served in the church gardens. Open house information and July timing are available from the M.S.A. Museum Society; (604) 853-0313. There is a small admission. The village is wheelchair accessible; private homes have steps.

Clayburn

Kilby Back Garden

Tretheway House

Location: North of Abbotsford on Highway 11; turn east on Clayburn Road.

Kilby Store Historic Park and Garden

Meticulous research has gone into recreating an exact 1920s yard and garden. Hollyhocks and sunflowers grow along the fence while the backyard has an old apple tree and a climbing platform. The store once housed the Kilby family and staff, and eventually grew into a small hotel, roominghouse and post office. Costumed animators add to its ambiance. Admission is charged. Plan on a "cuppa" at the Tea Room on site; (604)796-9576. The area is mostly wheelchair accessible.

Location: just off Highway 7 about 16 km (10 miles) west of Agassiz; follow signs.

Tretheway House and Garden

In 1920, B.C. lumber baron J.O. Tretheway (TRETH-oo-wee) built an arts-and-crafts-style bungalow. His wife, Mrs. Reta Tretheway and her sister-in-law complimented their fine home with an appropriate garden. Today, somewhat extended and roughly following 1920 standards, a climbing rose rambles up the chimney, rugosa roses cling to the arbor and a Montana Clematis drapes the gazebo. Near the house is Mill Lake, home to thousands of Canada geese. Information is available from the M.S.A. Museum Society, (604) 853-0313 or (604) 852-3722. Donations are appreciated. The garden and lake are wheelchair accessible; the house is not.

Location: 2313 Ware Street, Abbotsford.

A Brief History of British Columbia's Gardens

David Douglas, 1829

Dr. Helmcken's Healing Garden, 1850

Attracting farmers, 1890-1920

1740s Letters from the Czar's bureaucrats instruct Russian fur traders gathering furs along Canada's west coast to plant their own food gardens and 'assimilate' with the natives.

1784 Captain Cook stops at Nootka Sound. On-board naturalists gather "scientific" plant cuttings.

1791 José Monzino, naturalist-botanist for the Spanish Malaspina Expedition to Nootka Sound, collects seeds for Spain.

1792 Archibald Menzies, surgeon-naturalist on Captain George Vancouver's Pacific Northwest Expedition, collects Nootka Sound plant specimens.

1825 The Royal Horticultural Society sends Scotsman David Douglas to Washington, British Columbia and Alaska. Douglas introduces 200+ new species to Great Britain, including his namesake Douglas fir.

1827 Fort Langley, the last major Hudson Bay Company fur trading fort is established.

1842 The Wardian Case for transporting plants is used aboard British ships. Soon after, settlers in newly founded Fort Victoria receive shipments of bulbs, flowers, seedlings and fruit trees.

1850 Dr. Helmcken, Victoria's first doctor, grows a physick garden.

1853 HBC's Craigflower Farm near Victoria runs a commercial kitchen garden. An orchard is planted at Mission, B.C.

1858 To service prospectors, Thomas G. Earl (a.k.a. Earlscourt) sets up a kitchen garden and orchard near Lytton.

1862 Chinese prospectors grow kitchen gardens at Barkerville. Father Pandosy of Kelowna plants apple seedlings at his mission.

1867 The Canadian Pacific Railway starts a formal "Beautification of Farm and Town" program, planting kitchen gardens and flower beds around eastern railway stations. Railway demonstration gardens slowly spread west with the railway.

1868 The first agricultural show in Western Canada is held in Saanich near Victoria.

1870s "Closet" botanists, actually workers on the cross-Canada railway, collect pressed specimens and seeds and send them east. Today, many collections languish in local museums.

1888-89 Land is reserved for Stanley Park.

1890s Victoria's residents build a reputation for flowers.

1891 The Earl of Aberdeen attracts significant capital to irrigate the Okanagan Valley.

1896 Railway station demonstration gardens impress newly arriving immigrants. Part of the "Selling of Canada" program, they demonstrate that the West is "civilized."

1900 Victoria joins Canada's burgeoning Rural Cemeteries and City Beautification movement. Ross Cemetery becomes a "pleasure ground".

1907 First planned in 1904, Mrs. Jenny Butchart starts a flower garden in an abandoned quarry.

A Brief History of British Columbia's Gardens

*Railway Demonstration Garden,
ca. 1900*

*Riverview And Colony Farm,
est. 1905*

*VanDusen Outdoor Garden Show,
est. 1994*

1905 With irrigation projects in place, zealous English "gentlemen farmers" pour into the Okanagan.
1908 "Botany John" Davidson is hired to identify B.C.'s botanical riches. He grows representative specimens at Riverview and Colony Farm.
1909 Robert Douglas Rorison and his son expand Vancouver's commercial Royal Nursery.
1910s Railway demonstration gardens flourish around stations across Canada. Railway corporations employ staff horticulturists and landscapers; station masters receive trial seeds.
1916 The new University of British Columbia establishes one of Canada's first botanical gardens.
1919 Canadian soldiers returning from the war in Europe bring home "new" seeds. Enthusiastic housewives buy from American and British seed catalogues.
1922 Edward H. Lohbrunner, Victoria nursery owner and avid rock garden collector, is commemorated the Lohbrunner Alpine Garden at U.B.C. Botanical

Garden, Vancouver.
1925 Victoria opens Crystal Garden, a glass palace housing an indoor tropical garden and the largest water pool in the British Empire.
1926 On Vancouver Island, Dr. Frank Leith Skinner is Canada's foremost plant breeder.
1930s In Vancouver, Asian truck garden growers begin to develop an ornamental flower industry.
1935 In Cawston, the Shemilt family become commercial seed growers for the McKenzie Seeds Company.
1939 For $75,000, the federal government purchases Hatley Park Castle and garden.
1940s The Victory Garden movement keeps micro-agriculture flourishing while enlisted farmers are away. After 1945, Dutch floriculturalists immigrate and begin nursery operations in the West.
1960 Japanese landscape architect Kannosuke Mori designs Canada's first authentic Japanese garden, Nitobe Memorial Garden.
1966 Prime land is saved from development; Mr. VanDusen donates

a private bequest. In 1975, Vancouver's VanDusen Botanical Garden opens.
1978 Brian Minter establishes Minter Gardens, 90 minutes east of Vancouver.
1984 Funding is assembled to build a Chinatown landmark: Dr. Sun Yet-Sen Classical Chinese Garden.
1994 VanDusen Botanical Garden sponsors its first major outdoor garden show; it is said to emulate Chelsea's famous garden extravaganza.
1996 "Naturescape," a B.C. non-profit association, encourages municipalities to grow indigenous plants.
1998 Garden nurseries benefit from a burgeoning interest in home gardening as the "baby boomers" turn 50.

A Brief History of Lotus & Water Gardens

Surprisingly, the use of water as the fundamental ingredient in a garden has a much older history than do flowers. Whether in Islamic-Persian paradise gardens, reflective Chinese and Japanese ponds, cascading Italian extravaganzas, French formal marbled fountains, or central pools in courtyards, it is water that is the essential feature. Lotus blossoms were a logical addition.

- By 300 BC, Egyptian tomb paintings show gardeners tending lotus blossoms. The "Lotus of the Nile" hieroglyph represents the land of Egypt. Lotus blossom funeral wreaths are placed in tombs.
- In ancient Greece, water lilies dedicated to the nymphs are grown in grotto-like water gardens called nymphaeas.
- According to the Hindus, a

Lotus sits at the centre of the universe, growing from the navel of the Great God. Through practicing yoga, the highest level of consciousness is "the thousand-petalled

lotus."

- In the Buddhist world, the lotus flower grows in mud, but comes up white, and is called "sacred friend."
- In 1000 AD in China, Chou Tun-I writes an oft-quoted poem about water lilies.
- In 1849 in England, Mr. Paxton, gardener to the Duke of Devonshire, builds a greenhouse for the giant water lily *Victoria amazonica*. Discovered in British Guiana, it has leaves large enough to support a small child. Paxton raises one from a single seed.
- Throughout the 19th and 20th centuries, plant breeders try to unlock the secrets of colour in water lilies.

Communities In Bloom

The goal of Canada's "Communities In Bloom" program, an annual national beautification competition, is to involve municipalities across the country in competitive initiatives to improve the visual appeal of public spaces. Panels of judges crisscross Canada, rating participating municipalities on the originality of their landscaping, their green spaces, community involvement, environmental awareness, heritage considerations and tidiness.

Ottawa plays host to national awards ceremonies each November. 1996's National Award Winners by population were Toronto, Ontario (for provincial capitals); Calgary (for populations over

Canada 1996
Communities in Bloom
People, Plants and Pride
...Growing Together
Collectivités en fleurs
Citoyens et espaces verts en harmonie
... une société florissante

300,000); Burnaby, B.C. (for populations between 100,001 and 300,000); Lethbridge, Alberta (for populations between 50,001 and 100,000); Saint-Bruno-de-Montarville, Quebec (for populations between 20,001 and 50,000); Niagara-on-the-Lake, Ontario (for populations between 5,001 and 20,000); Virden, Manitoba (for populations between 1,501 and

5,000); and East Hereford, Quebec (for populations up to 1,500).

Toronto's mayor, Barbara Hall, tempered her win by donating 100 unique "Toronto" tulip bulbs to her competitors: St. John's, Charlottetown, Winnipeg, Regina, Edmonton and Victoria. Competitors and past winners from British Columbia include: Victoria, Vancouver, Burnaby, Richmond, Chilliwack, Kelowna, Surrey, Esquimalt, West Vancouver and Hudson's Hope. For further information, contact: Raymond Carrière, (514) 694-8871, fax (514) 694-3725; or Tony Kennedy, (905) 628-5944, fax (905) 628-6761.

Bill Coughlin, water garden devotee

Siberian iris

Lily Ponds Canada: Mission

Driven by a deep fascination for the iridescent world of water gardens, Mr. Bill Coughlin first began to collect water plants about 25 years ago. Like many before him, he came to understand the limited colour range available in hardy northern water lilies. However, over the last few years, hybrids have vastly improved and Coughlin's collection began to meet his high expectations. Proud of his wide-ranging specimens, he decided to open up his private acreage to the public. Still under construction in parts, 26 dug-out ponds cover an area of about 0.6 ha (1.5 acres.) In late June there is a showing of over 4,000 blooms among the 100 varieties of true water lilies, along with a co-flowering assortment of about 2,000 Japanese water irises and Siberian irises. Some have blooms the size of a small saucer. Bill invites visitors to view his ever-expanding water gardens in season and to buy high-quality, disease-free Canadian grown and tested water plants. From time to time, the Koi Fish Breeders Association utilizes his site for their shows. Best viewed from June through August; (604) 820-8164; the Water Lily Festival is in late June. This is also a commercial nursery. Tour buses run on Mondays only. Admission is granted with a donation. The wheelchair accessibility is fair to poor.

Location: 11202 Stave Lake Road, Mission; drive east on Lougheed Highway, left on Sylvester Road, follow the signs.

Elusive Watercolours

Water Lily

Without human intervention, water lilies come in one basic colour: white. For centuries, water gardeners were disappointed when they tried to hybridize the vibrant colours of tropical lotus blossoms into hardy northern water lilies. In 1858, the problem was tackled by Joseph Bory Latour-Marliac. He collected and cross pollinated species from all over the world. Finally in 1879, after years of failure, he discovered a successful hybridization technique and produced about 70 hardy coloured varieties still grown today. Unfortunately, in 1911 he took the secret to his grave. In 1912, Missouri Botanical Gardens' George Pring continued to propagate Marliac's stock, and several other breeders took up the challenge. One or two met with success—a matter of luck rather than skill. However, since 1990, hand in hand with a newfound enthusiasm for water gardens, its hybridizing colour secrets are being unlocked once again.

Minter Gardens entices visitors to explore a series of grand garden vistas interspersed with small, intimate spaces.

Minter Gardens: Bridal Falls

Set against the gleaming snow fields of majestic Mount Cheam is an inspired floral show garden,—the labour of love of garden personality Brian Minter and his dedicated staff. Located on 11 ha (27 acres) of rolling terrain, beautiful Minter Gardens features 11 theme gardens plus several waterfalls, ponds and aviaries. The garden's signature pieces are flower-covered armatures designed to resemble Victoria-era ladies in huge hoop skirts and an enormous floral peacock, fully 4 m (12 feet) long. The tree-dotted hillsides provide an ideal setting for several floral picture beds including the largest floral flag in Canada. Gently winding pathways progressively link the Rose Gardens, Formal Gardens, Alpine, Hillside, Fern and many more theme gardens. The living Evergreen Maze is a particular delight, where children giggle and grandparents pretend to get lost inside. A large collection of Penjing Rock is displayed in The Chinese Garden.

In spring, a rainbow of over 100,000 blooming tulips and daffodils are followed by a dazzling display of rhododendrons, azaleas, flowering Japanese cherry and magnolia trees. As summer progresses, mature perennial vegetation along with 200,000 or more annuals flood the gardens with torrents of colour. Hanging fuchsia baskets cascade at eye level and the wire armatures Minter calls "topiary sculptures" are ever-blooming wonders. As autumn approaches, a light dusting of snow cools

Brian Minter: Inspired Gardener

On a family outing to Harrison Hot Springs one Christmas morning in 1977, Brian Minter and his wife Faye ventured off the main highway and encountered a most interesting old farm site. The topography was so fascinating and the setting at the foot of a craggy 2,300 m (7,000 foot) mountain so uplifting, a once-in-a-lifetime dream was born. Brian set out to create a show garden to embody his ideals. Ground clearing began in October of 1978 and Minter Gardens officially opened July 1, 1980. "I knew an exciting show garden should have lots of experiences. So every 100 feet, we planned a new perspective," Minter says. "Large, colourful beds interspersed with gray shaded areas, even motion to contrast with stillness." Now a renowned gardening expert, Minter continues to advise gardeners through newspaper columns, radio programs and television specials. He and his wife operate two large country garden stores and continue to cherish their show garden.

Left: Complimenting a rare collection of Chinese rock miniatures hidden deep within the garden are fine examples of bonsai trees.

Mount Cheam and it contrasts brilliantly with the Japanese and vine maples firing up the hillsides with blazes of red, yellow and orange. As autumn gives way to winter rains, myriads of chrysanthemums and flowering kale finish off the season.

Minter Gardens' cheerful sights and fragrances are complimented by the tastes at their refreshment facilities. Though offerings may be as simple as soup, sandwiches and burgers, those making a day of it often order afternoon tea and a cheese scone, and stop to rest under the greenery on the patio. The Trillium Dining Room specializes in

sit-down gourmet lunches, including a generous Sunday Buffet Brunch between 11 a.m. and 2 p.m. Those in the know come prepared to buy as much cream and butter fudge as they can afford. Made fresh in Bloomers, it is nearly as famous as it is decadent. Nearby are two Garden Centres selling many of the plants so expertly displayed in the Gardens.

Phone for information: (604) 749-7191 or 1-888-646-8377. Wheelchair access here is excellent. Admission is charged. Minter Gardens is open daily from 9:00 a.m, but is closed seasonally from November through March.

Location: 52892 Bunker Road, Rosedale, in the Bridal Falls Resort area. From Vancouver (about 90 minutes by car), take the TransCanada Highway east toward Hope. Take exit 135 (the Harrison Hot Springs exit). The route is clearly marked, and there is good parking.

> *"Tickle the earth with a hoe—she laughs with flowers."*
>
> —Anonymous

Minter's Specialized Techniques

Armature draping

Carpet bedding

Clipped topiary

• **Armature draping** is a type of topiary garden art that starts with a wire form. Banked earth is packed onto the form for planting moss, greenery and flowers. Several outstanding "Victorian ladies" complement "Olive, the other reindeer." Armature draping was practised in the 1400s in Rucellai Gardens, Florence and in 1599 at Hampton Court, England. In B.C., it is found only at Minter Gardens.

• **Carpet bedding** was invented in the Victorian era, first appearing in the 1860s. Much as a tapestry maker embroiders threads, gardeners weave annuals and grasses into symmetrical designs. Named in England after knotted Turkish carpets, in France it is called *mosaiculture,* and in Germany, *Teppichgärtnerei.* Minter Gardens features Canada's largest floral flag and yearly logos dedicated to community events.

• **Topiary** (TOE-pee-air-ee), the art of clipping trees and shrubs into ornamental shapes, was first practiced in Roman times. From the 1500s, architectural forms like arches, pyramids or spheres on sticks were popular. By the late 16th century, almost every plant was subjected to the shears, regardless of its suitability. Topiary requires constant upkeep, making the specimens here even more delightful.

Minter's Penjing Rock Collection

During early Dynasties, when a sheltered Chinese emperor wished to know more about his newly conquered areas, he would instruct his literati (literate bureaucrats) to travel to the unknown lands and return with miniature models reflecting the areas' predominant landscape features—mountains, rivers and valleys. Using little rocks, sand and tiny tree sprigs, these table-top representations later became an art form in their own right.

The Chinese have long been fascinated with interesting rocks, which are the heart of all Chinese gardens. For centuries, nobles, poets and painters have been inspired by them. Giant limestone pieces are soaked in Lake Taihu—for up to 200 years, retrieved, and sold generations later as collector's items.

A feng shui expert analyzed this portion of the garden and balanced the ch'i or life force in order to display the authentic rocks to their best advantage.

The Emperor Song Hui Zong, reigning from 1101 to 1126 AD, had an enormous passion for strangely shaped rocks, even disrupting essential grain barges for his "rock convoys." When one transport sank, its cargo became a legend. In the 1500s, divers recovered it. The fabled limestone rock, now named "Exquisite Jade Rock," still stands in Mandarin Garden in Shanghai. Over the centuries, aristocrats have spent huge sums on bizarre rocks for their garden courtyards. Beloved single rocks are always named. When no appropriate limestones can be found, little alluvial rocks are piled into huge "false mountains."

Minter Gardens proudly displays an authentic collection of Penjing Rocks, the most comprehensive collection outside the People's Republic of China. The word penjing means "miniature." Placed in precise alignments, these little tableaux are arranged exactly as an Emperor would show off his territories to visiting dignitaries. This collection is a rare display for North American viewers.

Labyrinths Or Maze Gardens

To impress faithful churchgoers with the somber lesson that only one true path leads to righteousness, medieval churches once had huge mosaic labyrinths inlaid into their vestibule floors. However, during the 1500s, their purpose changed dramatically.

Maze hedges became a popular way to seduce young maidens. The hapless maiden was induced to enter the labyrinth, there to be pursued by amorous gentlemen. Upon encountering the disoriented young girl inside, the unaccustomed privacy afforded all sorts of engaging entertainment. For these fascinating pursuits, huge royal maze hedges were built in Spain, England, Italy Germany and France. In 1607, in Mantua, Spain, one had more than 3 km (2 miles) of twisted paths. At Versailles in 1774, the garden maze had 39 openings each with a fountain, a refreshment stand and topiary figures representing Aesop's fables; its total length was 0.75 km (0.5 miles). Today, maze hedges are used for innocent entertainment.

Information: Minter Gardens

Open	Daily at 9:00 a.m.
Year round	No, closed from November through March
Admission	Yes
Wheelchair access	Good; 90 per cent of the garden is setup for wheelchairs
Telephone	(604) 794-7191, fax (604) 792-8893, toll free 1-888-646-8377
Location	52892 Bunker Road, Rosedale, in the Bridal Falls Resort Area. From Vancouver about 90 minutes by car. Take the TransCanada Highway 1 east; take Exit 135 (the Harrison Hot Springs Exit). Follow the signs, easy access. Good parking.

Wedding Gardens: Fraser Valley

Garden weddings, always a favourite, have become exceptionally popular in recent years. For thousands of years, flowers and botanical items portraying fertility and life, have played a symbolic role in wedding ceremonies around the world.

In ancient Chinese wedding traditions, as the groom knelt at the family altar to prepare for his bride, his father placed a cap of cypress leaves on his head. During the ceremony itself, fertility was a common wish. The bride was showered with rice. Cups of tea, generally with two lotus seeds or twin red dates, were offered to the groom's parents, and the wedding bed was strewn with lotus seeds.

In the complex Hindu ceremony, there are several botanical moments. During the prarthana or prayer, the groom's and bride's fathers take three sips of purifying water with the right hand, then make offerings of incense, fragrant powders, light (fire) and flower petals. During the mangalashtaka—the eight blessings—the ritual concludes when guests throw colored rice over the couple. During the ceremony, the bride and groom face each other with long floral garlands in their hands. These are usually worn for the rest of the day.

Each year, almost 100,000 Japanese couples are married outside Japan in ceremonies with a decidedly Western flavour. Popular destinations include Guam and Hawaii, southern France, and the northwest coast of North

Traditional bridal ceremonies from many cultures, such as this Hindu wedding, are now part of the Canadian mosaic.

America, including Victoria and Vancouver. In a traditional Shinto wedding, there is an implied affirmation of the love of nature: cherry-blossom and maple-leaf viewing are important. Being in contact with nature is thought to place the couple in contact with true spirituality.

In Western traditions, flowers and botanicals also play an important role. The chapel or site is filled with floral arrangements and the white-clad bride carries an opulent bouquet, as do her attendants. No groom or best man would feel complete without a boutonnière.

Wedding Gardens in the Fraser Valley

These gardens have indicated that they welcome bridal parties and garden wedding photo shoots with advance notice. The public are welcome to watch the proceedings.

Centennial Park	Mission
Fraser River Heritage Park	Mission
Gardner Park	Abbotsford
Meadow Park Gardens	Pitt Meadows
Minter Gardens	Rosedale (Bridal Falls)
Williams Park	Aldergrove

Manning Park features a true sub-alpine wildflower meadow, accessible by car. Right: Stay on the paths; one false step can destroy 50 years' worth of growth.

Wildflower Reserves: Manning Park

Three exceptional wildflower viewing areas are located within a single provincial park.

Sub-alpine Wildflower Meadows: Reputed to be the only true sub-alpine meadow in the world accessible by car, this 2,000 m (6,500 feet) high meadow puts on two shows a year, each with well over a million wildflowers. In late May, as soon as the snow melts, wildflowers nod against the panorama of the Cascade Mountains. The first bloom features delicate whites and yellows: avalanche lilies, glacier lilies, and anemones. The second bloom features bright colours: paintbrushes, heathers, lupines and tiny elephant's head. It occurs for a 10-day peak period around the end of July. A well-timed visit is out of this world. Stay on the paths. Mountain weather is harsh, and all high altitude plants fight for survival.

Rein Orchid Reserve: Orchid lovers travel here to see the tiny white bog orchid, also

Rein orchid

known as the white rein orchid (*Platanthera dilatata*). Spikes of this vibrantly fragrant flower open in elongated clusters of 20 or more miniscule flowers along an upper stem. Growing in a well-marked, easy-access lowland moor meadow, the wild orchid blooms in July. Nearby Indian pipe orchids grow quietly. Local natives believed these brought them good luck when they gambled.

Wild Rhododendron Protectorate: Because of its rarity, the Pacific Rhododendron (Rh. macrophyllum) is protected by law. Occurring naturally, perhaps protected in a pocket from the last ice age, these wild bushes bloom in mid-June. All domestic garden varieties are crossed from wild varieties such as those found here. Five domestic hybrids have been created successfully using this particular wild variety, but only one is notable, Rh. Albert Close. It is found in VanDusen Botanical Garden.

The secret to arranging these wildflower adventures is timing. Both local weather conditions and variable conditions at high altitudes affect yearly bloom times. Phone the rangers at BC Parks, (604) 840-8836. They are pleased to tell you about this season's blooms. Be prepared to move quickly; nature waits for nobody. Park rangers schedule guided tours. Overnight options include staying at a comfortable lodge or camping; contact Manning Park Resort Lodge (604) 869-2911, or phone Manning Provincial Park for camping information (604) 858-7161. Each wildflower area is accessed via boardwalks and wide paths. A fee is charged to use the park. The area is wheelchair accessible but bumpy.

Location: Manning Park is 64 km (40 miles) east of Hope on Highway 3.

From blossom time to harvest time, apple orchards offer great viewing experiences and great tasting ones, too.

The Apple Farm: Yarrow

The folks who own this attraction have a fine sense of country living. Fundamentally a 4.3 ha (10.7 acre) high density espalier-like orchard, it grows 22 specialty varieties of apples. Gail and Klaus Berger's special Welcome House is filled with all sorts of crispy apple snacks, apple butters and apple jellies. The kitchen boasts a never-ending supply of freshly baked homemade apple pies; the farm help are dressed in calico aprons or fresh blue coveralls and best of all, the Bergers open their doors to visitors. Resident miniature goats, pigs and chickens are sassy and happy, and Klaus has rigged up a special train to snake down the apple rows to show off his Galas, Elstars, Fujis, Jonagolds, and other sunny varieties. Plan on bringing home some apples. It does a body good.

According to the Apple Nutrition and Benefits Survey, 1996, an average-sized apple has just 80 calories, is fat and sodium free, has five grams of fibre, and supplies 20 per cent of the daily fibre recommendation. Its fibre is soluble and helps lower blood cholesterol levels. Current research suggests naturally occurring chemicals found in apples, called flavonoids, may reduce the risk of heart disease and inhibit certain cancers.

Special orchard/garden events take place at apple blossom time—mid to late April—and at harvest time in September. A small admission is charged. The area is partly wheelchair accessible, but there are some steps. Phone for event times (604) 823-4311.

Location: TransCanada Highway 1 east, take exit 104, the Yarrow Cultus Lake cutoff; follow the signs for 3.5 km (2.2 miles); 4490 Boundary Road, Yarrow.

Apple Lore

• **In the** Garden of Eden, the serpent's seduction is associated with apples. Since Adam and Eve wore fig leaves, perhaps a fig would be more appropriate.
• In Greek lore, the god Paris—a handsome bachelor, chose as the most beautiful goddess the one who won a race for a golden apple.
• From Roman times to the present, it is unlucky to cut down an apple tree.
• In Celtic stories, a cut or bitten apple represents desire; modern-day advertisers continue to exploit this theme—teeth biting a red apple.
• For centuries, poets have compared apples' red and yellow hues to the sun.
• In the 17th century, it was widely believed that magical apple trees would be found growing around the Fountain of Youth.
• In Scandinavian lore, the gods ate golden apples and remained forever young.
• In many myths, the gift of an apple bestows immortality on its receiver.
• In Welsh legends, kings and heroes lived on after their deaths in Avalon—an apple-treed paradise.
.• As newcomers settled both Canada and the U.S., one of their first duties was to plant orchards. Apples were the most reliable crop.

Left: A delicious treat, apples are great for snacking or adding to recipes, and easy to carry along hiking or camping.

B.C. Interior Gardens

Heirloom elm trees, over 130 years old, stand by this original Waggon Roadhouse. Below: Afternoon tea at Ashcroft has been a tradition since the Cariboo gold rush, 1863.

Ashcroft Manor Teahouse: Ashcroft

In July 1858, in Fort Victoria on Vancouver Island, approximately 25,000 enthusiastic men suddenly arrived by steamship from San Francisco. Hardly stopping, they set out for "Frazer's" River. Easy-to-find gold continued to draw up to 40,000 hopefuls for years thereafter. Near Lytton, enterprising Thomas G. Earl (a.k.a. Earlscourt) immediately planted a kitchen garden,

imported fruit trees from the U.S. and sold produce to passing miners. But in 1861, when Dutch miner Bill Deitz dug a rich shaft, the focus shifted to hastily erected Barkerville. Under the guidance of the Royal Engineers, the primitive Cariboo Waggon Road quickly took shape. Mule trains and the the BX line stagecoach soon transported freight and people. The three week trip involved stops every eight miles at newly built Roadhouses, including Ashcroft. Records show that the men ate excellent three-course meals served on bone china. However, when beds ran out, they slept on the kitchen counters. In spite of these hardships, newly arriving Americans were impressed with the British civility they encountered. The Cariboo's low incidence of claim jumping and murders is attributed to decent food, a British sense of fair play, and the flamboyant Matthew Baillie Begbie—the Hangin' Judge.

Today, a sturdy white clapboard structure first built as a Waggon Roadhouse still stands proud. Built during the Cariboo's "golden year," 1863, its two enterprising English builders, Henry and Clement Cornwall, also planted two heirloom elms, still standing. The area is mostly wheelchair accessible. Phone for information, (250) 453-9983.

Location: Ashcroft Manor and Teahouse, 11 km (7 miles) south of Cache Creek, toward Vancouver, beside Highway 1 West.

Chinese Kitchen Gardens at Barkerville

Quietly, on the outskirts of Barkerville during the gold rush of 1858-1870, a tiny Chinese community silently reworked the tailings left behind by hasty miners. When winter threatened, most of Barkerville's population of 10,000 shipped out to the coast. The Chinese remained, planning for their own survival. At the far end of town on a mountainside, they planted a kitchen garden, hoping the ever-chilly winds would be kind. They sold their root crops to the 40 or so people who spent the winter here. The faint remains of these gardens can still be seen. Admission to Barkerville is charged. The area is mostly wheelchair accessible.

Location: Historic Barkerville is open in summer and is located east of Quesnel.

Left: The sight of even one cultivated garden plant from "home" made a deep impression on prospectors travelling to Barkerville's gold fields. Shown: Chinese cabin behind Ashcroft Manor.

135

Apiaries and Honey: Okanagan Valley

Canada, as a nation, is often associated with maple syrup. Eastern Canada, mostly Quebec, produces 75 per cent of the world's annual production or about 38 million pounds of the sticky stuff.

Bees and flowers participate in another sticky Canadian industry. Canada's beekeepers annually produce an astounding 72 million pounds of honey, one of the highest honey yields in the world. Average production in Canada per hive is 60 kg (130 pounds)—twice the world average. This results from a combination of long northern days, vast expanses of clover, alfalfa, canola and tree blossoms, and sophisticated management practices. Canada is the fifth largest world honey producer after China, the U.S., Mexico and Argentina.

As well as producing honey, bees pay a critical role in cross-pollination. It is estimated that it would cost the agriculture industry more than $100 million per year if bees were to disappear suddenly. Bees are vital to home gardeners and orchardists "hire" hives, moving 45 or more hives into their fields for 10 days at peak blossom times.

A Frueling rose and its insect visitor fuel an important industry. It takes this bee and 499 of its fellow workers a whole summer to make a pound of honey.

A pound of honey is a lot of work. According to Agri-Food Canada, it takes 500 worker bees working a full season to produce a single pound. The 500 bees each make about 25 trips per day; visit two million flowers; and fly a total of 88,500 km (55,000 miles). Busy!

The Canadian honeybee industry is self-sufficient, but it imports 150,000 quality queen bees from Hawaii, New Zealand or Australia each year.

Visitors are welcome to visit one or more honey operations and their busy little bees as long as the bees are in a good mood. All apiarists reserve the right to cancel tours on days the bees are "anxious." Please call ahead for tour timing.

Apiary Tours in the Okanagan Valley

Diggity Farm and Apiary mid-May to mid-September	Inquire when booking, Keremeos	(250) 499-5489
Orchard Blossom Honey & Bee Operations & Tours mid-May to mid-September	Upper Bench Road, Keremeos	(250) 499-2821
The Honey Farm Tours mid-June to mid-September	2910 North Glenmore Road, Kelowna	(250) 762-8156

Ginseng Production in B.C.

While it is still a bit of a novelty in western Canada, there is nothing new about ginseng. The Chinese were using it 5,000 years ago; by 37 BC, Koguryo, Korea had a monopoly on wild plants. Even the Romans used it. In Upper Canada in the 1700s, Jesuit priests showed pictures of wild ginseng to the Iroquois so that they could harvest it as they went about their hunting forays. At that time, European demand was so great, its export from Canada was second only to fur.

China's oldest written Herb Compendium (100 BC) discusses ginseng, claiming that it protects digestion, calms nerves, clears eyes, and makes the body light and agile. Today, ginseng is recommended as a tonic, rather than a specific cure. Scientific

Cultivating ginseng

studies show that it may reduce fatigue, stimulate the libido, and reduce blood sugar. Active research is underway to verify its anti-stress and possible cancer-suppressing benefits.

Ginseng is a major cash crop in British Columbia with a value pushing the $50 million mark. Most is sold in the Orient, and by the year 2000 the industry is expected to exceed the value of the B.C. tree fruit industry.

There are challenges:

ginseng plants are disease-susceptible, need arid growing conditions, and require four years from seedling to harvest. Each land plot must rest for 10 years between crops. In B.C., the root is cultivated under artificial shade canopies to produce a "cool" variety.

There are about 135 ginseng farms operating compactly on about 700 ha (1,730 acres) of land in B.C.'s interior. Ginseng is produced on leased properties around Lytton, Ashcroft, Williams Lake, Kamloops, Kelowna and Vernon. Watch roadside for the telltale black roofs. The root presently sells for about $88/kg and the seed for $110/kg. The ginseng business is financed by venture capital or public offerings. Information source: Agri-food Canada.

Water-wise Programs And Demonstration Gardens in the Interior

Xeriscaping or water-wise gardening is essential to B.C. Interior gardeners. Desert plants have characteristically small leaves that minimize evaporation. The following resources are available to the public. Phone for information.

Plants are tested for drought tolerance at the Summerland Research Station.

City of Kamloops Engineering Department, Xeriscape Demonstration Garden, West, Utilities Engineer	Contact: Mike Warren, McArthur Island, 7 Victoria Street (250) 828-3461, Kamloops Randi Derdall, Utilities Technician (250) 828-3395
City of Merritt Engineering Department, Water Conservation Education Program	Alec Hunchak or Gina Penny, (250) 378-4224
City of Vernon Engineering Department, Water Conservation Education Program	Eric Jackson, Environment Superintendent, (250) 545-8682 ext. 280
Project of the Penticton Naturalists Club, Plants of the Dry Interior Demonstration Garden; Okanagan University College	General Office, (250) 492-4305
Summerland Research Station, Agriculture and Agri-Food Canada, Dryland Garden in the Ornamental Garden	Brian Stretch, Gardens Manager, (250) 494-6385

The Monarch Butterfly: Its Plight

The monarch, *Danaus plexippus*, is a showy butterfly, famous for its spectacular migrations. Recent disasters and human pressures at wintering sites in Mexico have resulted in a catastrophic decline in their numbers. The Eastern monarch, found east of the Rockies from Alberta to New Brunswick, spends the winter in Mexico. The Western population, travelling the U.S. northwest and southern B.C., spends the winter in California. Western monarchs reach southern B.C. in huge numbers during summers with protracted heat waves. Breeding occurs in scattered locations, particularly in the Okanagan Valley and along the Fraser River.

As a gesture of good will during an Ottawa visit in June 1996, Mexican President Ernesto Zedillo and Governor-General Romeo LeBlanc released 100 monarch butterflies and planted an oyamel fir on the grounds of Rideau Hall. On August 2, 1996 in Toronto, Environment ministers from Canada, the United States and Mexico signed a tri-national agreement in the interests of the monarch butterfly.

Monarchs have an unusual defensive system called aposematic colouration. Adults exhibit bright orange, yellow and black patterns in order to warn potential predators that they are poisonous. They accumulate their poison as larva by eating poisonous milkweed. Hence, milkweed is vital to their survival.

In the early 1900s, monarchs' breeding areas were almost destroyed when the Great Plains were cleared. Native prairie flora used to include about 22 species of milkweed, all serving as larval host plants. Fortunately, as the West was turned into farmland, abandoned farms and clearings opened up in the East. Much of the population changed routes. However, when milkweed was designated an illegal noxious weed (to protect cattle), pressures mounted once again.

In October 1995, three areas in Ontario—Point Pelee, Long Point and Prince Edward Point—were designated Monarch Butterfly Reserves. No such protective areas exist in western Canada. Ultimately, the little creatures' survival depends on us. In parts of the U.S., rather than growing grasses along highway medians, wildflower mixes including milkweeds are being planted. Power line corridors are being maintained by cutting, rather than herbicide spraying, and Butterfly Gardens are part of many school curricula. Simple plantings in home gardeners' backyards, too, can play a role in ensuring the Monarch's continued survival.

Art in the Garden

Tiny planted courtyards inside old stone buildings, peacocks against yew hedges, lilies next to serpentine walkways, a single perfect rose: all these images form rich subjects for garden artists. There is a synergy between two of the oldest art forms—painting and gardens—and any number of community centres offer courses for amateur painters to try their hand at capturing the rich textures and colours of summer. Try your local community group for courses on either flower photography or garden arts. In addition, there are a number of craft outlets that cater to gardeners' needs.

In addition to butterflies and showy insects like praying mantis, this facility has an aviary.

Butterfly World: Kelowna

How did the butterfly come by its name? It depends who you prefer to believe. The Anglo-Saxons used the word *butter-floege* because they were familiar with the yellow brimstone butterfly. But in New World colonies, it was said these winged "witches" stole butter. In other languages, its name means "licker of milk."

Along with beliefs about souls going to heaven as butterflies, the ancient Greeks called them "psyche" meaning "soul." In Russian, they are called *bábochka* or "little souls." The Sioux Nation sensibly calls them the equivalent of "fluttering wings." The Danish *sommerfugl*, summer flyer, and the German and Yiddish *schmetterling*, seem to describe them well. But two all-time favourite sounding words are Indonesian, *kupu-kupu*, and Malaysian *rama-rama*.

Other origins are less pleasant. The Dutch word for butterfly describes the color of urine; a yellow drop from something that flies. In French, the Latin-derived word is *papillon*. French parking tickets are called papillons too, because they are big pieces of yellow paper that flap under the windshield wiper.

Watching butterflies, much like bird watching has become an enjoyable pastime. Since many natural butterfly habitats are being lost to urbanization, facilities such as this may be necessary for the preservation of the species. Okanagan Butterfly World is a well lit, enclosed, humid area with tropical plants and a good assortment of flutter-bys. Of course, this facility is also be noted for its outdoor bird aviaries, as well as its excellent tour programs. As with other butterfly facilities, photography is best when the area is fairly quiet and the best place to view the creatures is to find their feeding station. Admission is charged. The area is wheelchair accessible.

Location: 1190 Stevens Road, Kelowna.

Blossom and Harvest Times in the Okanagan Valley

The Okanagan region extends from Osoyoos in the south (corresponding to the earliest times listed), through the Central Okanagan including Summerland, Peachland, Kelowna and Penticton (about a week later), to the North Central Okanagan including Armstrong, Vernon and Enderby (about a week after that).

	Blossom Time	Harvest Time
Apples	Late April to mid-May	September to mid-October
Pears	Mid-April to early May	Mid-August to late October
Peaches	Mid to late April	Late July to mid-August
Apricots	Early to mid-April	Mid-July to early August
Cherries	Mid-April to late April	Late June to early July
Plums	Mid-April	Mid-August to late September

Lord and Lady Aberdeen

- **1847** John Campbell Gordon, the first Marquess of Aberdeen and Temair, is born in Scotland. In 1846, his father negotiated Canada's 49th parallel, forcing the Americans to concede Fort Victoria.
- **1857** Ishbel Maria Gordon Marjoribanks is born in London, daughter of Baron Tweedsmouth. Her uncle, First Lord Tweedsmouth of Guisachan, Inverness, Scotland, is the first breeder of golden retriever dogs—a breed developed between 1830 and 1890. One of the earliest is pictured here.
- **1877** Ishbel marries John Campbell Gordon. She becomes the Marchioness of Aberdeen. Her husband's title later escalates to Earl and Lord, and hers changes from Countess to Lady.
- **1887** Irish and Scottish lace and crochet workers are downtrodden. Irrepressible Ishbel aggressively assumes control of four organizations including the Royal Irish Industries Association. Workers gain from improved sales. Her personal popularity among the aristocratic class suffers.
- **1888** Britain's Dobbie Forbes Nursery releases a lacy white fuchsia in honour of the Countess of Aberdeen. See box p. 141.
- **1891** The Earl of Aberdeen buys Coldstream Ranch, 5,300 ha (13,000 acres) near Vernon. There, he plants 80 ha (200 acres) of hops for export to Britain. He builds luxurious Guisachan—his summer house.

In England, his investment alerts investor-immigrants to a potential "English country gentleman's fruit growing heaven."
- **1892** Countess Aberdeen builds Benvoulin Church in Kelowna. She believes women are the civilizing force in an untamed country.
- **1893** Lord Aberdeen becomes Governor-General. They move to Ottawa. She founds the National Council of Women of Canada. Organizing Irish lace displays at the Chicago World's Fair, she dramatically increases orders.
- **1894** Lady Aberdeen travels to Coldstream for the harvest. "Our hop-picking is a very picturesque sight....The Siwash Indians arrive, tents & all & settle down for a holiday time at the picking....Big boxes are given to them

numbered, & for each boxful they get $1—some get as much as $20 or $30 enough to keep them through the winter. At night they light fires & dance & sing & amuse themselves...."
- **1895** Lord Aberdeen is embroiled in political conflict.
- **1896** Lady Aberdeen bucks eastern medical opposition and founds the Victorian Order of Nurses (VON) for patients in remote districts—particularly the West.
- **1897** Lord Aberdeen resigns. Financiers fund major Okanagan irrigation projects.
- **1898** Lady Aberdeen organizes British volunteers to send free donated reading materials out West. Okanagan land values are $1 per acre.
- **1908** Okanagan land values are $1,000 per acre.
- **1910** Governor-General Earl Grey addresses the Royal Agricultural Society in New Westminster: "Fruit growing in your province has acquired the distinction of being a beautiful art as well as a most profitable industry. After a maximum of five years...the settler may look forward...to a net income from $100 to $150 per acre."
- **1911** Governor-General Earl Grey buys Lord Aberdeen's Coldstream property.
- **1934** Lord Aberdeen is buried at Harrow Weald in England, and five years later Lady Aberdeen dies in Scotland.

Guisachan House is now a fine dining restaurant and its gardens are open to the public.

Guisachan Heritage Park: Kelowna

In 1891, Lord Aberdeen, a member of the British House of Lords, became enchanted with the Okanagan Valley. After purchasing Coldstream Ranch in Vernon, he and his wife built Guisachan House in Kelowna. Lady Aberdeen then arranged to build Benvoulin Church (2279 Benvoulin Road) in the style of Crathie Kirk, Aberdeenshire, Scotland. All was in place for their retirement when the Earl was asked to be Governor-General of Canada.

In 1903, Patrick and Elaine Cameron purchased Guisachan House and turned it into a dairy farm. Mrs. Cameron was an avid gardener and her journals were used to restore the gardens to the style that was popular between the 1920s and the 1940s. The Cameron Milkshed is now a tiny gift shop. Because of this, locals sometimes call the site "Cameron Gardens."

A Gaelic word meaning "place of firs," Guisachan house was designed in the (East) Indian colonial bungalow style: one story high with generous verandahs. Today, it serves as an upscale restaurant and its surrounding one hectare (2.4 acre) garden is open to the public. The entrance is marked by an alpine rockery leading to a meandering path where mixed perennials form delightful banks of colour. There is a rose garden as well as a good selection of sumptuous irises. The highlight of the garden may be Dianthus X or "Lady Aberdeen" developed by Galbally Nursery, UK. Regrettably, another famous cultivar, the "Countess of Aberdeen" fuchsia, is not grown here. Near the back door, chef Georg Rider tends an herb garden and nearby is McDougall House, a square cut timber cabin visited by Lady Aberdeen, who wrote in her diaries about its "wild" gun-toting residents, the McDougall boys. Visitors may drop by the garden any time. Admission is free. The area is wheelchair accessible. Dining reservations are available at Guisachan Restaurant, (250) 862-9368.

Location: 1060 Cameron Avenue, Kelowna.

The Countess of Aberdeen

In 1988, the Countess of Aberdeen celebrated her centenary. It is difficult to believe that the enchanting lady is that old. She first came out in 1888 in Britain at Dobbie Forbes Nursery. Unfortunately, her parents are unknown, but F.m. alba was probably a part of her lineage. She is single, with a creamy white crown and a straight back. She blushes pink in the sun, but in the shade she is of the purest white. True ladies demand respect, and with deferential treatment she displays great charm and beauty.

Countess of Aberdeen

Of course, this "Countess of Aberdeen" is a fuchsia cultivar. With flowers as fragile as fine white china set off by a light pink star, she is easily the centre of attention in any hanging basket. The "Countess of Aberdeen" continues to appear on modern "Top Ten Fuchsias" lists. Many thanks to Kenneth Nilsson, fuchsia book author from Stockholm, Sweden. He provided both this photograph and the light-hearted overview. Additional thanks to the American Fuchsia Society, who provided more photos (not shown) of this lovely flower.

Happy Haunted Garden

Reputedly, haunted gardens in British Columbia include Century Gardens in Burnaby; Hatley Castle and Point Ellice in Victoria. Each reports tense emotional presences marked by unresolved circumstances. The haunting here at Guisachan House in Kelowna is a sound only—horses clopping, a carriage on a gravel path, and possibly a group of happy people. Those who have heard it have the distinct feeling a celebration is about to begin. When visiting this garden, seek out the entrance to the lane; it is slightly obscured. You too may feel or hear the uplifting presence of a mysterious horse carriage. The ghostly Doppler effect is reported on warm summer evenings, sometimes as the restaurant staff light

The Haunted Lane

candles on the verandah. The clip clop sounds occur inside the treed lane. If you hear it, and many have, you have the rare gift of clairaudience.

No definitive explanations for the sounds are known, though two vague clues exist. The Kelowna Archives has in safe-keeping the remembrances of Mrs. Allison, daughter of Lady Aberdeen. In 1954, she reminisced about the area's pumpkins "looking like they ought to contain Cinderella's coach"—an odd choice of words. The other is the irrepressible social crusading Lady Aberdeen herself. Burdened with the plight of starving lace workers in Ireland and Scotland, ridiculed for her social activism in Montreal and Toronto, she viewed faraway Guisachen House as an idyllic but sadly inaccessible part her life. Perhaps this is her sweetest dream, trying to come true.

Sorting out the Earls

• **Earl Grey** (1764-1845) was an actual person who, though he was prime minister of England under William IV, is better remembered for his namesake tea. Legends say the blend was given to him by a Chinese Mandarin seeking to influence trade relations. This particular Earl had nothing to do with the Okanagan.

• In 1858, Thomas G. Earl (a.k.a. Earlscourt) was the first person to set up a commercial orchard. Near Lytton, he grew fresh fruit and vegetables to sell to prospectors heading north to Barkerville—Earl the first Orchardman.

Which Earl?

Coldstream Ranch, Vernon

• In 1891, The Earl of Aberdeen (1847-1934) bought Coldstream Ranch and attracted investors. One year later, he became "Lord Aberdeen, Governor General of Canada" He was an aristocratic Earl—the Okanagan booster.

• In 1911, upon resigning as Governor General, Lord Grey (1851-1917) whose complete moniker was "Albert Henry George the 4th Earl of Grey Lord Grey" purchased Coldstream Ranch from the Aberdeens. This is the legendary Grey who established Canadian football's Grey Cup. This Earl of Grey has a relationship to the Okanagan, but none to Earl Grey tea. Pity.

Landscape rehabilitation experiments are ongoing.

Costumed animators work hard to keep the site authentic.

Heritage Gardens: Fort Steele

In the B.C. interior, near the city of Cranbrook, a masterfully restored pioneer settlement is designed to present five historic themes: the Kootenay Gold Rush; the establishment of the North West Mounted Police; Victorian Life in the 1890s; Logging Railways of the 1920s; and the development of agriculture. Unlike historic sites focused totally on their buildings, this particular facility also takes a well-researched look at regional gardens over the last 100 years.

During the 1890s, almost everyone needed a kitchen garden—the only affordable source of vegetables. The Chinese community, living alongside the rough prospectors, were particularly zealous vegetable-growers. The first settlers tested seeds and passed on their knowledge in an effort to ensure a good first harvest and a better one each season thereafter. Donald J. Berg, a historical animator says, "They grew a greater variety of vegetables than we do now and developed methods to extend their home grown bounty throughout the year."

Sharon Remple, M.A. in Conservation Studies, Historic Landscape and Garden Restoration England, has been championing the Canadian garden restoration movement since 1988. An Alberta resident, she travels throughout western Canada to research and restore period gardens. She also locates Victorian plants and seeds; rediscovers traditional practices; teaches organic farming and sustainable agriculture; and consults on historic landscape designs. Contact Sharon Remple, Box 1406, #194-3803 Calgary Tr., Edmonton, AB T6J 5M8. Doing a recent stint at Fort Steele, Remple verified the Victorian-era flower bed design and colour theory, located sources for historic flowers and vegetables, and even helped to break the ground for planting.

By bringing historic gardens to life, Fort Steele's historic animators add a new dimension to public education. No public program demands more work than the complexities of historical organic agriculture. Perhaps this is why such garden programs are relatively rare.

The programs are richly rewarding. "Nothing gives back as much as does the agricultural program," a staff member says, "The splashes of colour, the horses straining in their harnesses, the aroma of stews and baking pies, many of the sensory inputs on the site all stem from the gardens." The staff dress in costume and are knowledgeable about the history they recreate. Closed in winter. Phone for information (250) 426-6923. Allow a full day to visit. Admission is charged. The area is mostly wheelchair accessible.

Location: Fort Steele is 16 km (10 miles) northeast of Cranbrook on Highway 95.

Hudson Bay Company Gardens

The thought of Hudson's Bay Company (HBC) posts conjures up romantic images of voyageurs and Indian scouts, not of sweating gardeners. However, the HBC was probably responsible for the first organized gardens in Canada. As early as the late 1600s, HBC field men were writing letters begging for seeds to supplement their meagre supplies. At first, their company directors refused on the grounds that gardening would take away from their other work. Later, they relented but made a series of mistakes sending out unsuitable seeds. Bravely, the New World's would-be gardeners pressed on. Hardy varieties were eventually found and as early as 1715 in York, HBC employee James Knight noted a small yield of turnips from "some seeds in the garden." As the anti-scurvy qualities of produce came to be recognized, company directors tolerated vegetable patches, but still worried about men spending too much time in the garden. Company directors extolled the virtues of self-sufficiency and money-saving wherever possible, but forbade their men to grow anything they considered frivolous or luxurious. Rye was a common unauthorized crop.

HBC gardens were simple affairs, little plots fenced off from the animals and severely hampered by the extreme cold of the northern outposts where furs were gathered. A HBC entry from York on June 14, 1732 complains of the ground still being frozen. Because of their tolerance to frost, turnips were common, as were radishes, lettuce, peas, and a form of hardy cabbage called

In this recreated Hudson Bay Company garden located at The Grist Mill in Keremeos, rye is one of the "unauthorized" crops.

Old HBC employee letters indicate rye was grown.

"colewort." In its day, any luck with the harvest was viewed as joyous bounty.

Times changed. By the early 20th century, the company routinely provided its field workers with compulsory garden manuals, tips on frugality, and cold weather growing tips.

Information sourced from *Fur Trade Gardens in The Prairie Garden* by Tim Ball, University of Winnipeg.

Recreated HBC Garden Plots Growing in British Columbia Today

Craigflower Farmhouse	Victoria
The Grist Mill Heritage Site	Keremeos
Fort Steele Heritage Site	Near Cranbrook
Fort St. James Heritage Site	North of Vanderhoof

"Grist" is a well-known word in the East, but not as well understood in the West. It means "grain ground in a mill."

Grist Mill animators work hard to take care of all the gardens.

The Grist Mill Heritage Gardens: Keremeos

Imagine a bag of flour harvested from Red Fife, a wheat variety last popular in the 1890s. Imagine a field of wheat grown from seeds found at a 6,000-year-old archaeological site in Persia. Think of a Hudson Bay trader, alone in the vast wilderness, rejoicing at his small rye harvest. Picture an orchard with odd-looking apples like the Richter Banana Apple—varieties grown more than 100 years ago. See a Victorian-era lady carefully tending her precious imported flowers. Turn your curiosity to a huge melon growing so fast in midsummer, you can hear it grow! Turn on your appetite and

> *"Prince's [flour] mill is running day and night and cannot keep up with the demand."*
>
> — Similkameen Valley Newspaper, 1881

take in the smells of home baking exactly as they were 150 years ago. All these experiences are available at The Grist Mill, the last surviving flour mill from the pioneer settlement period in British Columbia. Flour was an important staple and wherever grain-growing occurred, a flour mill cropped up. Though several dozen water-powered mills were once scattered throughout B.C., Prince's mill, built in 1877, is the only full reconstruction in operation.

Of great interest to garden aficionados, the vital growing history of the Similkameen Valley is presented here in an extensive series of well-researched heritage show gardens, fields and orchards.

Costumed animators work the site in summer, planting and tending gardens, nursing orchards and wheat fields and adding to the delightful ambiance. Bakers turn out trays of delicious goodies made from harvests of wheat, herbs, vegetables and fruits. The Creekside Tea Room overlooking the gardens serves tea, lemonade and goodies made from heritage Thatcher Wheat flour.

Passing through the Visitor Centre, the first stop is the Heritage Garden area. Here, visitors can see and touch gardens from various eras. The Victorian Circle Gardens burst into bloom in midsummer. They contain unusual ruffled flowers and peonies while the plain root cellar sits sedately to one side, awaiting the root bounty. Perhaps the most intriguing planting is the Zucca melon bed. From one single seed, an entire melon patch emerges. A type of bottle gourd, the Zucca was once used to make candied peel for the baking industry. One remarkable seed produces scores of melons weighing from 27 to 60 kg (60 to 100 pounds) growing so quickly, you can hear the plant pop and crackle. In a single summer day, individual melons can put on up to one or more kg (1 to 2 pounds) and the vines can grow up to 15 cm (6 inches). Needless to say, the Zucca is hard on soil fertility and needs a revitalized plot each year. Because of this, it went out of fashion, and only a few brave gardeners grow one today. These adventuresome gardeners purchase their seeds from The Grist Mill and participate in a rare "garden sport." Each September, the Annual Great Zucca Reunion is held here, so home gardeners can boast about their results.

Word of the Living Museum of Wheat has spread excitedly among certain groups. Alberta farmers and others who visit the site rave over the Heritage Wheat Fields and

Specialty flours ground in the mill and fruits from the surrounding orchards combine into delicious goodies in the Creekside Tea Room at The Grist Mill. Try the homemade lemonade.

varieties like Red Fife they thought were extinct. Many of the heritage grain fields were planted from odd pounds of old seeds found stashed in paper bags in an Agriculture Canada facility in eastern Canada.

A visit to the mill itself, with its great waterwheel

Heritage Garden Beds Growing at The Grist Mill

Sub-garden	Era	Description
• Hudson's Bay Co. (HBC) subsistence plot	1861-1871	Plants noted in HBC letters and archives. See page 142.
• Frank Richter's kitchen garden	1880s	His homestead garden was a marvel for its time; varieties from 1880s seed catalogues.
• Julia Bullock-Webster's flower diary	1890s	Avid botanist, spirited watercolour artist, true Victorian-era lady, this Keremeos woman authored beautiful diaries. Flowers noted in her diaries are grown here. See Victorian-era style, page 9.
• "New" orchard interplantings & heritage apple orchard	1910s	Experimental fruits and vegetables were grown to determine commercial viability. Here are some of the experiments.
• Shemilt family farm seed growers	1930-1960	This family from Cawston grew seeds for the MacKenzie Seed Company. Here is their 1938 garden and its onions. See page 120.
• Similkameen ground crops	Present	Locally irrigated crops include ginseng, melons, peppers, squash etc. as they are grown today.
• Flowers of the Grand Gardens	Heirloom plants	Flowers from Lang's Nursery once went to The Butchart Gardens and Legislative Buildings; offspring of these exact flowers are grown here.
• Herb garden	Ancient to ongoing	For centuries, knowledgeable gardeners have grown these gardens for food, dyes and medicine. See page 36.
• Victorian-era favourites	1850-1900	Open pollinated flower varieties are grown in a circle, exact varieties from the Victorian era. See page 9.
• Living Museum of Wheat The harvest is made into special flours at the mill.	4000 BC -1921	Living wheat fields include thriving Einkorn, its seeds recovered from a 6,000-year--old site in Persia; Red Fife (1842); Marquis (1892); Ladoga (1886); Thatcher (1921) and more.

The Three H's of Old Gardens: The Grist Mil

Heirloom — Most valuable of all, these are actual old-era plants, bushes, or trees that escape destruction and survive intact. In effect, we inherit them. — Rare Richter Banana Apple tree developed by pioneer Frank Richter

Heritage — Offspring from an era's original plants: shoots, seeds, cuttings. — Heritage wheat fields planted with saved seeds from Canada's national gene bank

Historic — True to a certain time period; a plant exactly like the species that would have grown during an era. Research is required to source these. — Victorian circle garden: settlers' old varieties from 1860s and older

Heritage Gardener Extraordinaire, Cuyler Page

Special tribute must be paid to this attraction's dedicated curator and caretaker, Cuyler Page. Through his efforts and those of his dedicated staff, the flour mill machinery itself was laboriously reconstructed, fitted together and restored; the mill, water wheel and heritage gardens are kept in tip top shape; the time consuming task of organic gardening using old methods is made into an inspired art.

Curator and Caretaker, Cuyler Page

turning and the wooden shafts whirring, is best if a guide is available to explain the details. Periodic demonstrations of flour-making occur each day. The Exhibit Building details the innovative work carried on at the site and displays the meticulously worked watercoloured pages from the Flower Diary of a gracious Victoria-era lady, Julia Bullock-Webster.

After tea or lemonade and a home-baked treat, many visitors depart with a genuine promise to become ambassadors and spread the word about this outstanding facility and the fruits, flowers, vegetables and grains not seen elsewhere for decades. Research into heritage gardens is a continuous process and expert Sharon Remple (noted in the entry on Fort Steele, page 143), worked extensively at this site. Heritage and historic seeds are available from the gift shop.

Information: The Grist Mill

Type	A reconstructed old flour mill, water wheel and heritage gardens with costumed animators; a Provincial Heritage Site
Size	4.8 ha (12 acres)
Time allotment	2 hours
Open	9:30 a.m. to 6 p.m. or dusk
Year round	No, closed from November through April.
Best seasons	Summer, autumn
Sub-gardens	Hudson Bay post gardens, kitchen gardens, flower diary gardens, early orchard, herb garden, Victorian-era flower garden, Zucca melon, Living Museum of Wheat
Additional facilities	Working heritage flour mill, working water wheel, visitor centre, tea room, home baking, gift shop, pet refreshment area, heritage seeds for sale. Note: Guard your pets against heat suffocation in a hot vehicle. Ask the staff for details.
Events	Ongoing interpretation programs; craft workshops, lectures, concerts
Admission charged	Yes
Wheelchair access	Mostly accessible
Guided tours	Guided tours available
Telephone	(250) 499-2888
Location	R.R. #1, Upper Bench Road, follow the signs, Keremeos.
Nearby attractions	Fruit stands

The sound of water is part of the Japanese garden experience.

Kasugai Japanese Garden: Kelowna

Dedicated in 1987 as a gesture of friendship between Kelowna and its twinned city, Kasugai, Japan, the beauty of these gardens is intended to link the two cities and their people in a symbolic way.

Asia's Kasugai city is Japan's cactus capital. Each year in April, the entire population of Kasugai celebrates Sakura Matsuri (cherry festival) and Shokubutsu-en Matsuri (arboretum festival.) It is also home to Ochiai Park and its Tower of Water, considered one of Japan's top 100 city parks as well as the Kasugai Arboretum and Botanical Garden.

Kasugai's city sister shares many common interests with Kelowna. Overlapping interests include peaches, cherries, green belts, gardens and parks.

Kelowna's Kasugai Japanese Garden was designed by local farmer, Mr. Roy Tanaka in the tradition the kawaramono, "riverbank workers." Originally the outcasts of society, their wonderful works gradually elevated them to the status of professional garden architects during the Muromachi era (1393-1568.) This one ha(3 acre) strolling pond garden is meant to be a serene harbor of peace for visitors to enjoy shakkei, and its interpretation of nature in miniature. The rake and the sandbox are provided for visitors; the tradition is to emulate waves. Sansui is one of the most important metaphysical concepts underlying both garden art and painting and the sansui in this garden is well worth a lingering visit. Admission is free. Hours are limited. The area is mostly wheelchair accessible.

Location: North of Queensway or off Water Street, behind City Hall, Kelowna.

Japanese Garden Vocabulary

Chozubachi	Stone hand-washing basin
Dosen	The layout of the pathway between the gate and the front entrance of a building
Ginshanada	Literally, "silver sand, open sea"; raked white sand
Go-shintai	Literally, "abode of a deity"; may be an unusual rock, tree, mountain or waterfall
Hako-zukuri	Topiary technique of clipping trees into a box shape
Hashi	Bridges
Ikedori	To draw the outer landscape into the garden by "capturing it alive"; this term for "borrowed landscape" is much older than the more recent term, shakkei
Karesansui	Dry landscape garden; gravel and stones used to represent water
Karetaki	Rocks and sand arranged to resemble a waterfall
Kazari-musubi	Decorative rope knots on little bamboo fences
Ma	A sense of place
Nokiuchi	The area under the eaves of a building; very important in relating the garden space to that of the building
Nosuji	Artificial, low mound with a gentle slope
Samon	Ripples and other patterns formed in shikisuna
Sansui	Juxtaposing a mountain and water landscape
Sawa-watari ishi	A type of stepping stone for crossing water
Shakkei	Imitating the outlines, shapes of larger landscapes
Shikiri-gake	Totally walled garden
Shiki-ishi	Paving stones
Shikisuna	Beds of coarse sand or gravel with rake
Shinsento	An unearthly mountain island in a mythical sea
Takeho-gaki	A fence constructed from bamboo branches
Taki	Waterfalls
Tobi-ishi	Stepping stones
Toro (niwa doro)	Large stone lantern at garden's emotional centre
Yarimizu	Murmuring stream flowing past a stone lantern

Left: Kelowna's Japanese Garden is located behind high walls.

Polsen Park: Vernon

Polson Park was donated to the City of Vernon by Samuel Polson, a land speculator and developer. The park is home to Luc Girouard's cabin, probably the city's oldest building and a reflection of the early settlers' days.

Within the park is a small, unkempt Japanese garden, dedicated to the City of Vernon by the Japanese Canadian Community Association. Challenged by its proximity to an old high-school and buried deep in a heavily shaded part of the Park, it is a shame to see this garden deteriorate. At one time, this park also displayed an excellent example of Victorian carpet bedding, a great working floral clock made entirely of clustered flowers. At the time of this writing, it too was in disrepair. Admission is free. The area is wheelchair accessible.

Location: Fronts on Highway 6 and Highway 97 south.

Under the tenets of feng shui, the roof-line shape of this shelter is considered favourable, though its placement near a rushing steam may be washing its favourable chi away.

Orchards and Gardens of Abundance: Okanagan

The old fashioned hospitality involved in trying out the products of August's and September's harvests is as refreshing as any cultivated garden experience can be. Today, many orchardists will guide you through their rows of lush fruit trees. Roadside fruit stands are plentiful and beckon you to enjoy the fruity abundance. Besides tree fruits and fresh produce, many offer homemade jams, apple butters, syrups, jellies, pies, juices and cider. Listed here are modern orchards, some with accompanying flower gardens open to visitors.

Facility Visits	Location	Phone
Appleberry Farm May through September	3193 Dunster Road R.R. #3, Kelowna 20 ha (50 acres)	(250) 868-3814

Heritage Garden, orchard tours, beehives, 55 fruit products, apple pie and coffee, heritage apple orchard, blossom and harvest festivals, petting animals, tea on the porch overlooking the orchard

Kelowna Land & Orchard (KLO) April through October	2930 Dunster Road, Kelowna 57 ha (140 acres)	(250) 763-1091

Original KLO farmhouse gardens, advanced fruit tree and environmental techniques, branded albino apples, spectacular view, guided orchard tours, orchard wagon rides, farm-gate sales, fresh juice

Davidson Orchards July through December	3097 Davison Road, Site 2, Comp 10, R.R. #4, Vernon 20 ha (50 acres)	(250) 549-3266

U-pick cutting flower gardens, heritage orchard displays, petting animals, spectacular view, vegetable plantings, self-guided orchard tours, produce market, apple pies and desserts, fresh pressed juice

Many visitors are surprised by the beauty and elegance of Summerland's ornamental gardens—part of a serious research facility. Monarchs are frequent visitors here; see page 136.

Ornamental Gardens: Summerland

Since 1916, visitors have enjoyed visiting this hilltop arboretum and the six hectares (15 acres) of mature flower gardens accompanying Agriculture Canada's Research Station. The garden's stately Superintendent's Residence, built between 1920 and 1926, is described as an English country cottage but at 4,000 square feet and styled in the manner of the Canadian prime minister's official eastern "cottage," it belies its humble title. Near the cottage is an arboretum including a Brewer's Bruce weeping beech, male and female deciduous Kentucky coffee trees, ponderosa pines and ash trees. The rambling garden overlooks Trout Creek Canyon Gorge, Giant's Head Mountain, a Kettle Valley Railway trestle and outstanding panoramic views of the surrounding Okanagan valley.

With only 290 mm of rain available to them each year, home gardeners appreciate the xeriscape landscape garden. The iris collection is exceptional, as is the rose garden in June. One variety, "Eddies' Crimson," was bred by western Canadian breeder, Henry Eddie of H.M. Eddie & Sons. A small plaque designates a scion of the first fruit tree planted in the valley. Horticulturists continue to turn to the large collection of crab apple trees bred for disease resistance, taste or fruit quality.

Please bring a brown bag lunch to enjoy under the ash trees as there are no on-site water or food outlets. Phone (250) 494-7711. Admission to the gardens is $2 or more by donation. The area is wheelchair accessible.

Location: off Highway 97, midway between Penticton and Summerland.

Meaningful Flower for Canadians: the Fleur-de-Lis

Of all the flower figures in mediaeval heraldry, none is more widespread than the three-pronged fleur-de-lis, a symbol of royal power and divine protection. Poorly translated into English as "lily," the symbol actually refers to the iris flower. Starting with King Clovis in 496 AD, the symbol was adopted by the kings of France as the royal insignia. France's fleur-de-lis flew over early holy land crusades and when battles were

won, it was embroidered into royal robes, carved onto furnishings and even embossed into armor. Louis XIV, the "Sun King" shown here, was one supporter. As France's conquests spread, his soldiers carried fleur-de-lis flags to many nations. Today it remains a powerful symbol for the Canadian province of Quebec. By coincidence, many Quebecois come to the Okanagan region to work as farm labourers. Perhaps the proliferation of sumptuous irises in the Okanagan has magnetic appeal.

151

Small Gardens: Okanagan

Gibbard Gardens: Naramata

"Daffodils, that come before the swallow dares, and take the winds of March with beauty" – William Shakespeare, 1564-1616. Since 1956, this privately owned garden on a lovely sloping site overlooking Lake Okanagan has been growing an estimated 43,000 daffodils along with an assortment of crocuses and rhododendrons. Today, it is periodically open to the public, particularly on Sunday afternoons near Easter or in mid-April. Phone for details (250) 496-5255. Admission is charged; proceeds are donated to the Penticton Hospital. Wheelchair accessibility is fair.

Location: 13.6 km (8.5 miles) from Penticton, on Arawana Road in Naramata.

Gibbard Gardens

Memorial Rose Gardens: Okanagan Falls

"Where fall the tears of love, the rose appears ..." – Nicklos Muller, writer, 1809-1875. Timing visits to gardens-in-bloom can be a science, though most people know the best time for roses is generally mid-June through mid-July. This tiny rose garden packs 190 hybrid tea roses into a small space not too far from a quirky mix of antique stores, restored heritage buildings and small town shops. The gray stucco of the nearby building is strangely disturbing, though the roses don't seem to mind. Admission is free. The area is wheelchair accessible.

Location: On Main Street (Highway 97), Okanagan Falls.

Memorial Rose Gardens

S.S. Sicamous and Rose Gardens

Veendam Gardens

S.S. *Sicamous* and Rose Gardens

Permanently moored between the south end of Okanagan Lake and the north end of Skaha Lake, the S.S. *Sicamous*, was the last fruit-transporting sternwheeler to operate on Okanagan Lake (1914-1936). Visitors are welcome to look around the sternwheeler, beached here since 1951 and presently under restoration as a Provincial Heritage Site. Next to the sternwheeler is a small rose garden. Several roses are planted here in honour of Penticton's sister city, Keda, Japan. In the centre of the garden is an analemmatic timepiece, an elegant word for a modern sundial that indicates both the time and the date. The timepiece does have one drawback: it does not adjust for daylight saving time.

Location: S.S. Sicamous Park, Penticton.

Veendam Gardens: Kelowna

"When a man gives a woman a tulip, he wants her to know by the colour of it that his heart is on fire, and by its black base that his heart is burnt to a coal."—Omar Kyan, 1700s.

These gardens located within City Park are a tribute to Kelowna's sister city in the Netherlands, Veendam. The gardens display a multitude of perennial and annual floral displays clustered around a cenotaph, a monument to those who have given their lives in war. Tulips and spring flowers give way to manicured beds of particularly colourful annuals. Admission is free. The area is wheelchair accessible.

Location: City Park, Kelowna.

Special Interest Visits: Okanagan

Giant Ponderosa Pine: Lake Country

One fun way to verify the identity of this orange-barked pine tree is to scratch the bark and sniff deeply. A distinctive vanilla aroma arises. Growing only in British Columbia in zones of low summer rainfall, the pondera's soft lumber was once used to construct fruit crates. It grows nowhere else in Canada. Between 1930 and 1950, many black and white Hollywood movies such as "Rose Marie," "O'Rourke of the Mounties," and others about the Great Northwest a.k.a. Canada, were filmed in the U.S., where these trees are common. With such lingering images, many late night movie watchers are surprised at the ponderosa pine's relative rarity in Canada. The B.C. Registry of Great Trees lists the largest ponderosa pine in Canada at 41 m (134.5 feet) in height and 4.82 m (15.8 feet) around. There is a taller specimen in California, but it has a smaller crown spread. A core sample indicates that B.C.'s giant sprouted about 1635.

Location: From the Kelowna airport, travel north on Highway 97, take Beaver Lake Road for 6 km (4 miles), then take the first dirt road to your left, cross the cattle guard, and in 0.5 km (0.3 miles). You will see the giant ponderosa.

Wildflower Nursery: Oliver

Dried flowers are a good way to keep summer's colours alive well into winter. A wreath is a good first project because its flowers do not need long stems. Drying flowers in the microwave, with or without the help of silica gel, can preserve everything from roadside weeds and grasses to straw flowers, hydrangeas, yarrows and goldenrods. Some items such as holly berries, nuts and the exceptionally large pine cones found throughout the Okanagan take on new life when coloured with spray paints. Golds, silvers and white are particularly festive at Christmas time.

Colourful hills of herbs and wildflowers are grown here in Oliver, and after harvest, individual flowers are dried and prepared for distribution to hundreds of floral and craft suppliers. Visitors may drop in and tour the colourful grounds, bring a picnic lunch, and browse the General Store. Guided tours are available with notice, phone (250) 495-7678. This is a commercial outlet. The area is wheelchair accessible.

Location: Wildflower Nursery, Off Highway 97, south on No. 20 Road, Oliver.

Native Plant Availability

A good source for finding Canadian-bred seeds and plants is The Canadian Plant Sourcebook by Anne and Peter Ashley. Over 20,000 hardy plant listings are keyed to the Canadian nurseries that sell them. Correspondence concerning purchasing this 416 page paperback book should be sent to: The Canadian Plant Sourcebook, 93 Fentiman Ave., Ottawa, Ontario K1S 0T7. The authors can also be reached by telephone (613) 730-0755, by fax (613) 730-2095, and by e-mail at: apashley@worldlink.ca.

Special Interest Visits: Okanagan

British Columbia Orchard Industry Museum: Kelowna

Located in Kelowna's first designated heritage building, the Laurel Packinghouse, this museum explores the region's transformation from cattle ranching and grain growing to orchards. For about a hundred years, apples, pears and other tree fruits have been grown and shipped from British Columbia. The industry began with the sale of surplus fruit from backyard orchards. By the 1890s, land agents in the Okanagan Valley and parts of the West Kootenay region were advertising 5 and 10 acre orchard lots for sale. Within a generation after the introduction of irrigation, much of the parkland landscape of the southern interior was transformed from wide open cattle range to manicured, symmetric orchards. Displayed here are all aspects of B.C.'s fruit industry—irrigation, spray pest control, picking, pruning, packing, and processing. Information, (250)763-0433. A small admission is charged. The area is wheelchair accessible.

Location: 1304 Ellis Street, Kelowna.

Father Pandosy Mission: Kelowna

The Immaculate Conception Mission, established by French Oblate missionaries Charles Felix Pandosy (1842-1908) and Father Pierre Richard, was one of the first places to grow fruit trees in the valley. In 1862, three years after they established the Mission, the Fathers planted a small orchard of

BC Orchard industry Museum

Father Pandosy Mission

perhaps six trees, derived from seedlings brought to the Okanagan from St. Mary's Mission at Mission, B.C. The orchard suffered the vicissitudes of winter, drought and disease and was destroyed by a fire, which also burned the old Mission house. One mighty tree survived until the great winter freeze of 1955-56. A seedling apple from the surviving tree was propagated and a specimen tree and commemorative bronze plaque stand at Summerland's Agriculture Canada Research Station; see page 149. In 1967, seedlings from the

surviving tree were replanted at the Pandosy Mission. Father Pandosy is occasionally compared to America's "Johnny Appleseed." However, credit for the fruit industry goes to dozens of ranchers who first planted fruit trees, then the many pioneers who settled the valley. The good Fathers' few trees were no doubt a contributing factor. Admission is granted with a small, non-obligatory donation. The area is wheelchair accessible.

Location: 3685 Benvoulin Road, Kelowna.

Agriculture Canada's Research Station (ACR) in Summerland

ACR has lately developed a number of innovations for improving the marketability of B.C. products.

• A technology in collaboration with a British Columbia winery, leading to a new natural sparkling wine of the champagne type now for sale in Canada

• An evaluation of modified-atmosphere packaging to keep fruits fresher longer

• Answers to the appearance of haze in apple juice, a harmless but costly problem

• Increased productivity techniques for tree fruits and grapes

• New cultivars for raspberries, strawberries, apples and sweet cherry

A lovely afternoon tea at the Store House is available indoors as shown, or in their delightful garden.

Tea in the Garden: Vernon

While there are many places in the Okanagan where a well-presented cup of tea would be much appreciated, there are but few dedicated tea houses where tea is as it should be. Wine sampling is the great pastime now perfected in this region. There are a few establishments serving tea in Penticton and Kelowna (Gathering Room Tea House, 3045 Tutt Street). The notable one is Douglas and Jane MacKenzie's The Store House, a tearoom and garden of extraordinary ambiance. Afternoon tea or light lunches are served alternately in the pleasant indoor atmosphere of their Victorian-era house, or on sunny warm days, outdoors in a delightful summer garden. Tea in this garden brings to mind Dorothy Frances Gurney's poem, "The kiss of the sun for pardon, /The song of the birds for mirth, /One is nearer God's heart in a garden, /Than anywhere else on earth." If you enjoy tea in the traditional style, or a light lunch with tea on a sunny warm day, this rare experience is worth a special trip to Vernon. Dried flower arrangements and garden accessories are available in the gift shop. The garden is wheelchair accessible. Phone for information, (250) 549-4540. Closed Sundays.

Location: The Store House, Victorian Gift Shop and Tea Room, 3001-25th Street, Vernon.

About Tea Tasting

Tea Type	Proper Additions	Details	When
English Breakfast	Milk preferred; lemon if you must; never both	Most popular blend of fine black teas, including Keemun tea	Any time
Irish Breakfast	Much sugar and room temperature milk; never cream	Full bodied, robust, second grade teas blended from Assam tea base	Morning good; afternoon, if you must
Caravan	Milk, much sugar or honey; also take jam tarts. If no milk, then a lemon studded with cloves.	Combination of China and India black teas; first created in Imperial Russia	Afternoon
Lemon Tea	Clear or with sugar and lemon; no milk; basically meant for iced tea	Second or third grade blends with added artificial flavour to cover deficiencies; a North American invention	Afternoon
Earl Grey	Taken clear; no exceptions	Smoky tea with a hint of sweetness; the second most popular tea in the world	Any time
Darjeeling	Always taken clear; milk destroys its best qualities	Grown in the best mountain areas of India; unique, full bodied but light with a lingering aroma reminiscent of Muscatel	Afternoon only
Oolong	Taken clear; no exceptions; take with cucumber sandwiches & madeleines	Elegant; the "champagne of teas"; Formosa Oolongs grown in Taiwan are the highest grade; a cross between green and black teas;	Afternoon only
Green tea	Clear; some people have a genetically based taste aversion to it	Unfermented tea; the proper preparation for Japanese green tea is beyond the ability of most	When properly served during a Zen tea ceremony
Keemun	Clear; or sugar and/or milk; never lemon	Chinese black mellow tea with a subtle yet complex nature; the "burgundy of teas"	Any time

The Never-ending Quest for Unique Garden Stylings

In terms of B.C.'s regional garden style at present, there is a definite push toward naturalistic gardens utilizing indigenous plants. When this trend has come to the fore in the past, its inherent lack of excitement against the backdrop of familiar scenery usually condemns it to an early demise. If history repeats itself, a skillful variation—likely a new fad with strong elements of contrived excitement—will quickly take over. Though each change in garden style arouses pitched passions, "fashion" in gardens over the past 300 years has swung like a pendulum between free-flowing naturalism and architectural formality.

What does B.C.'s future hold? Though we are reluctant to admit it, humans long to see exaggerations of nature. In spite of talented landscapers who ramble on about "imitating" nature, show gardens actually overemphasize, manipulate, change and tidy up what is truly natural. After all, once cleared, the ultimate "natural" is a weed-filled vacant lot.

What humans long for is somewhat "unnatural." We fence off a piece of ground followed by skillful organizing, balancing, simplifying or redressing whatever the environment provides in overabundance. Too much desert? We long for water gardens. Too much rock? We stuff plants into crevices. Too much naturalness? We plunk in a manmade sculpture. Too

Canadian aboriginal art offers one potential Western garden trend.

much horizon? We interrupt it with trees. Too much sun? A pergola covered in rambling roses is one answer. Too many plants? A dry, crunchy gravel path looks inviting. Too much green all round? A splash of red flowers, or an all-white garden draws favourable comment. The otherworldly serenity of nature in an Asian garden, for example, is created by humans who excavate and rearrange every square millimetre of the site until it meets the criteria of an ideal philosophical flow. It reminds us of nature (the famous "borrowed landscape" concept), even though it does not replicate reality.

Surprisingly, the greatest challenge in finding a unique

style in British Columbia may be its abundance of sensational scenery. To imitate nature in this region seems futile, as gardens pale in comparison. So far, the greatest design work has been done by emulating, synthesizing and reworking the horticultural heritage of B.C.'s many ethnic immigrants. Only one tradition has been largely ignored—B.C.'s aboriginals. Their art traditions flow from a ten-thousand-year head start living on the land. Their symbolic forms beg investigation in the B.C. garden context.

In Europe, where western garden trends have begun for the last 300 years, Chelsea's Flower Show (England) is presently agog over gardens with historical themes such as a Regency Garden or a Privy Garden. The names "le Nôtre," "Repton" and "Olmsted" are common currency at smart dinner tables. However, in British Columbia at the moment, the will to create unique garden styles is weak; the rediscovery and preservation of wilderness (quite rightly) is the great push. The pendulum will swing. Perhaps British Columbia's greatest contribution to the world of gardens remains a twinkle in the genes of someone yet unborn.

Okanagan wine growers spent many years determining which grapes do best on their land. Numerous public events matching excellent foods and outstanding wines in exceptional settings are part of the Okanagan experience.

Vineyard Tours: Okanagan

Vineyards are a special type of garden—apparently one of mankind's oldest. Currently in British Columbia, there are approximately 40 assorted wineries offering internationally respected wines. Of the three regions where these wineries are located, the Okanagan Valley is the largest. Monolithic Okanagan Lake and its moderating effect on the blistering afternoon heat of the semi-arid desert is primarily responsible for the favourable micro-climate. Neighbouring vineyards produce notably different wines.

More than 20 years ago, government research helped determine which grapes would ripen properly. The main grape varieties today include: Auxterrois, Bacchus, Chardonnay, Chasselas, Ehrenfelser, Gewurztraminer, Riesling and Pinot Blanc.

At present, British Columbia's winemakers are especially noted for their crisp, fruity, clean-tasting white wines and full-bodied dessert wines. Whites are often made in the German tradition—off-dry and slightly sweet. Dessert winemakers favour the French Sauterne style "late harvest." Lately, German-style ice wines—grapes picked and crushed while frozen—have become exceptionally popular. Though a few great red Pinot Noirs have been bottled, B.C.'s reds are inconsistent in quality. Further work is under way.

Along with know-how, British Columbia has a strict quality control program. The hard-to-earn VQA symbol, Vintner's Quality Alliance, is modeled on France's high quality AOC program and Italy's DOC. VQA certification is strictly enforced.

At the end of a vineyard tour, enjoy the fruits of the harvest.

Vineyard Safaris and Festivals in the Okanagan

Perhaps considered a special type of garden, the relationship between vineyards, gardens and the pleasures of life is many centuries older than any of us alive today. Enjoy the bounty of the land.

Okanagan wine route wine and vineyard tours	May through October	Brochure available at any B.C. Liquor store, or the Okanagan Similkameen Tourism Association, 1332 Water Street, Kelowna BC, V1Y 9P4, (250) 860-5999, fax (250) 861-7493 or 1-800-661-2294
Two annual Okanagan wine festivals	Early May & again in September	Program available at the Wine Festival Office, 185 Lakeshore Drive, Penticton BC, V2A 1B7; 1-800-972-5151; or 1-800-665-0795; (250) 861-6654

"Give me the splendid silent sun with all his beams full-dazzling, Give me juicy autumnal fruit ripe and red from the orchard, Give me a field where the unmowed grass grows, Give me an arbor, give me the trellised grape."

— Walt Whitman, American poet, ca. 1850

157

Index

Reference

About the Author

Pat Kramer writes special interest guides for travellers who yearn to discover western Canada. She writes not for the generic "tourists," but for travel connoisseurs who delight in well planned trips filled with hidden wonders that are often overlooked.

Because she is a part-time tour director, her books concentrate on visitors' best-loved attractions. The result of her research, interesting stories and colourful photographs is a pleasurable guide on B.C.'s public show gardens.

It will be difficult for you to read about all these places without wanting to get up and see for them for yourself. "My greatest revelation in writing this book, "she says, " is the depth of tradition that has shaped the gardens here in British Columbia."

Among Kramer's other special interest guidebooks are: *Native Sites in Western Canada* and *Totem Poles*, (both of which have been translated into German), and *B.C. for Free and Almost Free*. Current and upcoming Altitude releases by Pat Kramer include *Quotes on the Rocks* and *Vancouver SuperGuide*. Pat maintains several Web pages using keywords from her book titles. E-mail is at these sites. Come visit.

Photography Credits

All photos are by the author, Pat Kramer except those noted below. Kramer's photos have appeared in *Native Sites in Western Canada* and *Totem Poles*, both by Altitude Publishing, as well as in *Beautiful British Columbia* and many educational and tourism promotions. Pat wants to pay special tribute to her father, James Holditch, who was an avid gardener and flower photographer.

Thanks are also due to Jo Curran, who travelled to Costa Rica for a photo of a monarch butterfly, and to all the generous animators, curators, gardeners and horticulturists whose valuable input resulted in the first compilation of information on B.C.'s public gardens. The European gardens were photographed by the author. Particular thanks is directed to the Omotesan-ke Doko-ka Tea School. Their secrets are revealed on page 28. The Victorian-era Conservatory is located near Kensington Palace, London. Anne Lindsay, foremost cookbook author in Canada, appears on page 69b. The French Formal Garden, page 61, no longer exists. It was part of Paris' Louvre.

B.C. Orchard Industry Museum: 154
B.C. Provincial Archives: 11, 35,47b,48,49,140
Burnaby Village Museum: 29b
Chris Cheadle: 67
James Holditch: 12, 17, 25d, 79b, 100, 151d
Jo Curran: 138, cover butterfly
Kelowna Archives: 142
London Wax Museum: 53
Vancouver City Archives: 94, 97b,
Vancouver Public Library Archives: 29a